about this book

Not so very long ago, kids didn't need cookbooks written just for them. But times have changed. Our lives are a lot busier, and children often do not learn to cook the way they once did, at their parents' sides.

That's why I think a book like this one is so important. It teaches kids the basics any good cook should know. Even better, it features foods that not just kids but the whole family will enjoy making and eating. So parents can cook from the book right alongside their children.

In fact, it's a good idea—and a safety-conscious one—for grownups to read and use this book with their kids. Start by reviewing the basics at right and on the following pages. Then pick your favorite recipes and begin cooking. Everyone, young and old, will be surprised at how much fun and how satisfying it is to prepare good food.

Chuck Williams

ready to cook?

Here's what every kid should know about getting started in the kitchen.

• Ask an adult to stay in the kitchen with you and to lend a hand when needed.

• Tie back long hair to keep it from getting in your way.

• Roll up your shirt sleeves and wear an apron to keep your clothes clean while you cook.

• Wash your hands with warm water and soap before you handle food and equipment.

• Rinse and dry off fruits and vegetables before you use them. Handle delicate-skinned fruits and vegetables, like berries and tomatoes, gently. Give tougher-skinned produce, like potatoes and carrots, a good scrub.

• Clear off and clean a space big enough to work comfortably.

• Clean up work surfaces and equipment as you use them. Being neat as you cook makes for easy cleanup and easy cooking.

• Work slowly and have fun!

WILLIAMS-SONOMA

the kid's cookbook

a great book for kids who love to cook!

general editor **Chuck Williams**

recipes and text Abigail Johnson Dodge

photography **Leigh Beisch**

Oxmoor House®

contents

how to follow a recipe

• Before you do anything else, carefully read the recipe from start to finish.

• Make sure you have enough time to complete the recipe without rushing.

• Assemble all the equipment called for in the recipe.

• Gather the ingredients called for in the recipe.

• Prepare your ingredients as they are described in the ingredient list. This may include measuring and chopping, and is called *mise en place* (see definition below).

• Begin cooking.

mise en place

Pronounced **meez ahn plahs,** this phrase is commonly used in professional kitchens. It means "put in place" and refers to having all of your ingredients measured and ready to use as the recipe directs. You might need to peel an apple, chop an onion, or shred cheese. Having your *mise en place*—your ingredients ready—helps to make following a recipe easy and fun.

playing it safe

• Always ask an adult for help when you have questions.

• Clean up spills as soon as they happen.

• Clear away equipment as soon as you're done using it.

• Take special care when handling knives and other sharp tools.

• Stay in the kitchen while the stove or oven is in use.

• Use dry pot holders or dry oven mitts to handle hot pots and pans. Heat travels through damp or wet pot holders or oven mitts.

• Let hot pots and pans cool before putting them in the sink or cleaning them up.

super-easy recipes!

A good number of recipes in this book call for only a few ingredients and are very easy to make. They are marked with ✳ next to their name at the start of each chapter and on the recipe pages, too. These recipes are perfect for beginning cooks.

measuring

When you cook, it's important to use ingredients in the correct amount. Just think of pancakes made with too much salt or of cookies made with too little sugar! It's also important to measure or keep track of time. Have a set of measuring spoons and cups, a liquid measure, and a kitchen timer on hand to measure ingredients and time as a recipe directs.

dry ingredients

• Spoon the dry ingredient into a dry measuring cup or spoon.

• Do not pack down the ingredient, unless it's brown sugar. Brown sugar is always measured firmly packed.

• Level off the ingredient with the back of a table knife.

wet ingredients

• Put the liquid measuring cup on a flat surface.

• Bend down so the measuring lines are at eye level.

• Pour in the liquid until it reaches the correct measuring line.

butter

• Use the measuring lines marked on the butter wrapper as your guide.

• Set the stick of butter on a cutting board.

• Line up a small, sharp knife on the appropriate measuring line and cut down through the butter to cut off the correct amount.

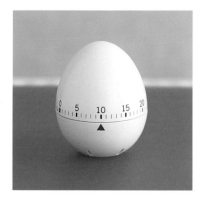

time

• Use a kitchen timer to keep track of time when cooking.

• Don't rely on time alone to know when food is done. Well-written recipes provide times and visual clues for knowing when food is ready.

shapes and sizes

Ingredients can be cut into different shapes and sizes. Generally speaking, small, skinny pieces cook quickly and big, chunky pieces cook slowly. Use this photo to help you identify the shapes and sizes described in the recipes that follow.

sticks

sliced

neatly chopped

shredded

adding up

dash = 2 or 3 drops

pinch = amount you can pick up between your thumb and forefinger

3 teaspoons = 1 tablespoon

4 tablespoons = $\frac{1}{4}$ cup

5 tablespoons + 1 teaspoon = $\frac{1}{3}$ cup

1 cup = 8 fluid ounces

2 cups = 1 pint

2 pints = 1 quart

4 quarts = 1 gallon

4 ounces = $\frac{1}{4}$ pound

8 ounces = $\frac{1}{2}$ pound

12 ounces = $\frac{3}{4}$ pound

16 ounces = 1 pound

here's how

the basics are tasks repeatedly used in cooking. Whether you need to scrub fruits and vegetables, break an egg, or shred some cheese, doing it correctly is important. Look no further. Here's how!

fruits & vegetables

rinsing

1 Rinse fruits and vegetables under cool running water.

2 Scrub tough-skinned items, like potatoes, with a vegetable brush.

3 Rinse them again and pat dry with paper towels.

eggs

cracking

1 Tap the middle of the egg firmly against the rim of the bowl.

2 Hold the egg above the bowl.

3 Gently pull the two halves of the shell apart.

cheese

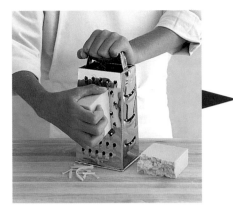

shredding

1 Hold the grater-shredder firmly with one hand.

2 Keeping your fingers away from the holes, rub the block of cheese against the shredding holes.

3 Continue shredding the cheese, moving from top to bottom.

pasta

testing

1 Remove a piece of pasta from the pot of boiling water with a slotted spoon.

2 Let the pasta cool slightly.

3 Bite into the pasta. If it's tender but still firm, it's done.

gelatin

plumping

1 Soak the gelatin in cold liquid until it is plump.

2 Dissolve the plumped gelatin over heat.

3 Add the dissolved gelatin to the mixture that needs to be set.

here's how

fruit is available all year long and comes in many shapes, sizes, colors, and textures. Some fruit is sweet and some is sour. Here's how to prepare fruit for cooking and eating. Always rinse and dry fruit before using it.

pears & apples

peeling

1 Steady the pear on a cutting board.

2 Using a vegetable peeler, peel away the skin by pushing the peeler away from you.

3 Keep turning and peeling the pear.

coring

1 Hold the apple stem side up and cut it in half.

2 Cut each half in half again.

3 Cut away the core from each piece.

strawberries

hulling

1 Hold the berry at its pointed end.

2 Cut across the top of the berry to remove the stem.

3 Slice the strawberry or leave it whole.

apricots, peaches, plums, nectarines & cherries

pitting

1 Cut the peach in half along the indentation.

2 Gently twist the two halves apart.

3 Lift out the pit with your fingers or a spoon.

lemons, limes, oranges, tangerines & grapefruits

zesting

1 Rub the orange over the small holes of a box grater-shredder.

2 Rub off only the colored part of the skin.

3 Stop when the spongy white pith underneath begins to show.

here's how

vegetables can be tender or tough. Some taste great raw. Others are best cooked. Here's how to prepare some common vegetables for cooking and eating. Always rinse and dry vegetables before using them.

herbs

chopping

1 Place the leaves in a small pile.

2 Hold the knife with one hand and rest the fingers of the other hand on top of the knife.

3 Gently rock the knife back and forth to chop the herbs.

carrots & potatoes

peeling

1 Hold the carrot at the stem end.

2 Using the vegetable peeler, peel off the skin by pushing the peeler away from you.

3 Keep turning and peeling the carrot.

onions

chopping

1 Cut the onion in half lengthwise and peel away the skin.

2 Trim away the stem end of the onion.

3 Cut each half lengthwise into slices without cutting through the root.

4 Hold the onion slices together at the root end.

5 Be sure to keep fingers out of the way.

6 Cut across the slices to make chopped pieces.

garlic

chopping

1 Separate the head of garlic into cloves.

2 Smash a clove with the palm of your hand and peel away the skin.

3 Cut the clove lengthwise and then across into very small pieces.

here's how

baking means to cook with hot, dry air in an oven. Cookies, cakes, and pies are all foods that you bake. Here's how to handle a few basic techniques that are commonly used in baking.

baking pans

preparing

1 Rub the inside of the pan with a piece of butter.

2 Sprinkle a small amount of flour into the pan.

3 Tilt the pan and tap lightly until the bottom and sides are evenly coated with flour. Dump out the excess.

doneness

testing

1 Use pot holders to take the pan out of the oven.

2 Stick a toothpick into the center of a muffin.

3 Gently pull out the toothpick. If it comes out clean, the muffins are done.

batters

scraping bowls

1 Steady the mixing bowl with one hand.

2 Run the spatula slowly around the inside.

3 Or turn the bowl, keeping the spatula in place, to scrape the batter from the sides.

butter & flour

cutting together

1 Put the butter into the bowl of flour.

2 Using two table knives, cut through the mixture.

3 Continue cutting through the mixture until crumbs form.

heavy cream

whipping

1 Pour the heavy cream into a bowl.

2 Using an electric mixer, whip the cream just until soft peaks form.

3 Turn off the mixer. Lift the beaters and check that the peaks hold their shape.

breakfast & lunch

* = super-easy recipe!

- ❑ measuring cups & spoons
- ❑ cutting board & table knife
- ❑ small saucepan
- ❑ wooden spoon
- ❑ pot holder

- ❑ mixing bowls
- ❑ table fork
- ❑ rubber spatula
- ❑ griddle
- ❑ metal spatula

banana pancakes

INGREDIENTS

- 6 tablespoons (¾ stick) butter
- 1½ cups all-purpose flour
- 2 tablespoons sugar
- 2½ teaspoons baking powder
- ¼ teaspoon salt
- 1 small, very ripe banana, peeled
- 1 cup milk
- 2 eggs
- ½ teaspoon vanilla extract

  maple syrup and sliced bananas, for serving

1 Cut the butter into 3 equal pieces. Put 2 of the butter pieces in the small saucepan and set the remaining piece aside. Set the pan over medium heat and stir with the wooden spoon until melted, 1 to 2 minutes. Using the pot holder, remove the pan from the heat and set it aside to cool.

2 In a medium mixing bowl, combine the flour, sugar, baking powder, and salt. Mix with the fork until well blended.

3 Put the banana in a small mixing bowl. Mash with the fork until almost smooth. Add the milk, eggs, and vanilla and stir with the fork until well blended. Pour the banana mixture and the melted butter into the flour mixture. Mix gently with the rubber spatula until the batter is just blended. The batter should still be a little bit lumpy.

4 Put the griddle over medium heat until hot. To test if the griddle is hot enough, flick a drop of water onto it. It is ready if the drop dances quickly and evaporates. Put half of the remaining butter onto the griddle and spread it with the metal spatula. Drop the batter by ¼ cupfuls onto the griddle, spacing them about 3 inches apart.

5 Cook until a few holes form on top of each pancake and the underside is golden brown, about 2 minutes. Carefully slide the metal spatula under each pancake and turn it over. Cook until the bottom is golden brown and the top is puffed, 1 to 2 minutes longer. Using the spatula, transfer the pancakes to a serving plate.

6 Repeat with remaining batter. Serve the pancakes while still hot with maple syrup and sliced bananas.

Makes twelve 4-inch pancakes

ripe bananas
are easy to mash

lots of
blueberries
make these
muffins
extra delicious

EQUIPMENT

- ❏ measuring cups & spoons
- ❏ cutting board & table knife
- ❏ small saucepan & pot holder
- ❏ wooden spoon & table fork
- ❏ paper liners & 12-cup muffin pan
- ❏ mixing bowls
- ❏ rubber spatula
- ❏ large spoon & toothpick
- ❏ oven mitts & cooling rack

big blueberry muffins

INGREDIENTS

½ cup (1 stick) butter, cut into 3 equal pieces

2 cups all-purpose flour

½ cup plus 2 teaspoons sugar

1 tablespoon baking powder

½ teaspoon salt

1 cup milk

1 egg

¾ teaspoon vanilla extract

1 cup blueberries, rinsed and dried

1 Put the butter pieces in the small saucepan and set over medium heat. Stir with the wooden spoon until melted, 1 to 2 minutes. Using the pot holder, remove the pan from the heat and set it aside to cool.

2 Preheat the oven to 375°F. Put the paper liners in the 12 muffin cups.

3 In a medium mixing bowl, combine the flour, ½ cup sugar, baking powder, and salt. Mix with the table fork.

4 In a small mixing bowl, combine the milk, egg, and vanilla. Using the same fork, beat until well blended.

5 Add the milk mixture, melted butter, and blueberries to the flour mixture. Using the rubber spatula, stir gently until the ingredients are just blended.

6 Spoon equal amounts of the batter into the muffin cups. Sprinkle the extra 2 teaspoons sugar evenly over the tops.

7 Bake the muffins until they are golden and have risen nicely, 18 to 20 minutes.
To test, insert the toothpick into the center of a muffin. If it comes out clean, the muffins are ready. Using oven mitts, remove the muffin pan from the oven and place it on the cooling rack. Let the muffins cool for at least 15 minutes before removing them from the pan. Gently turn the pan over, letting the muffins fall out onto the rack.

Makes 12 muffins

- ❏ measuring spoons
- ❏ cutting board
- ❏ small, sharp knife
- ❏ 2 small mixing bowls
- ❏ 2 table forks
- ❏ small nonstick frying pan
- ❏ pot holder
- ❏ heatproof flexible spatula

cheese and herb omelet

INGREDIENTS

2 **tablespoons cream cheese, at room temperature**

1 **tablespoon chopped fresh chives, thyme, basil, or parsley**

2 **eggs**

1 **tablespoon water**

pinch of salt

pinch of pepper

1 **tablespoon butter**

1 In a small mixing bowl, combine the cream cheese and herbs. Mash with a table fork until blended. Set aside.

2 In the second small bowl, combine the eggs, water, salt, and pepper. Using a clean table fork, mix together until just blended. The eggs should not be foamy.

3 Add the butter to the frying pan and set over medium heat. When the butter is melted and starts to foam, swirl the pan to coat the bottom with the butter. Pour the eggs into the pan and cook until the edges begin to look set, about 45 seconds. Holding the pan steady with the pot holder, use the spatula to lift up an edge of the omelet and tilt the pan slightly toward that edge. The uncooked egg in the center will run onto the pan bottom. Continue to cook and repeat the lift-and-tilt movement 2 more times at other points around the edge.

4 When the center of the omelet no longer looks runny but is still moist, drop teaspoonfuls of the cream cheese mixture over half of the omelet. Slide the spatula under the other half of the omelet and flip it over the cream cheese half.

5 Gripping the pan handle firmly with the pot holder, hold the pan over a serving plate. Tilt the pan slightly and let the omelet slide out of it onto the plate. Serve immediately.

Makes 1 serving

omelets are great
for breakfast or lunch

a great way to start the morning

EQUIPMENT

❑ measuring cups & spoons
❑ cutting board
❑ small, sharp knife
❑ electric blender
❑ 1 or 2 tall glasses

fruity morning shakes✳

INGREDIENTS

1 **container (8 ounces) vanilla yogurt**

2 **teaspoons sugar**

6 **strawberries, stems cut off**

OR

1 **small ripe peach, pit removed and cut into chunks**

OR

1 **cup blueberries**

ice cubes (optional)

1 Put the yogurt and sugar in the container of the electric blender. Add your choice of fruit.

2 Put the lid securely on the blender. Make sure it's on tight! Hold down the lid with your hand (so it isn't forced off by the spinning liquid) and turn the blender on to high speed. Blend until thick and smooth.

3 Fill 1 or 2 glasses with ice cubes, if you want your shake frostier, and pour the shake into the glass(es). Serve immediately.

Makes 1 or 2 servings

EQUIPMENT

- ❏ measuring spoons
- ❏ cutting board
- ❏ sharp knife
- ❏ small saucepan
- ❏ pot holder
- ❏ medium mixing bowl
- ❏ table fork

easy egg salad sandwiches

INGREDIENTS

3	eggs
3	tablespoons mayonnaise
1	tablespoon milk
1	small celery stalk, thinly sliced
	salt and pepper
4	slices marble rye or your favorite bread
2	lettuce leaves
2	slices tomato

1 Put the eggs in the small saucepan and add water to cover. Set the saucepan over high heat and bring the water to a boil. Reduce the heat to medium-low and simmer the eggs for 12 minutes.

2 Using the pot holder, carefully place the saucepan in the sink and run cold water over the eggs for about 1 minute to cool them off. When they are cool enough to handle, tap the eggs gently all over to crack the shells. Peel away the shells and put the eggs in the mixing bowl. Throw away the shells.

3 Using the table fork, mash the eggs against the bottom and side of the bowl until small chunks form. Add the mayonnaise and milk. Mix with the fork until blended and a little creamy. Stir in the celery and season to taste with salt and pepper. If not using immediately, cover with plastic wrap and refrigerate.

4 Line up the bread slices on the cutting board. Divide the egg salad in half and pile each half on a slice of the bread. Top each mound of egg salad with a lettuce leaf and a slice of tomato. Top with the remaining bread slices and cut the sandwiches in half with the sharp knife.

Makes 2 servings

an old-fashioned favorite

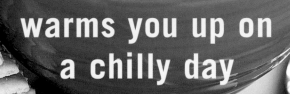
warms you up on
a chilly day

EQUIPMENT

- ❏ measuring cups & spoons
- ❏ cutting board & sharp knife
- ❏ can opener
- ❏ electric blender
- ❏ medium saucepan
- ❏ wooden spoon
- ❏ pot holder
- ❏ table spoon
- ❏ ladle

creamy tomato soup*

INGREDIENTS

3   small green onions

1   can (14½ ounces) diced tomatoes

1   cup chicken broth

¼   cup milk

1   teaspoon sugar

   salt and pepper

   crackers, for serving

1 Place the green onions on the cutting board and cut off the root end with the sharp knife. Peel away the outer layer of skin. Cut the white part and about 2 inches of the green into thin slices and set aside.

2 Open the can of tomatoes with the can opener and pour the contents into the container of the blender. Add the chicken broth, green onions, milk, sugar, ½ teaspoon salt, and a pinch of pepper. Put the lid securely on the blender. Make sure it's on tight! Hold down the lid with your hand (so it isn't forced off by the spinning liquid) and turn the blender on to medium speed. Blend until very smooth.

3 Pour the contents of the blender into the medium saucepan and set the pan over high heat. Bring the soup to a boil, reduce the heat to low, and simmer, stirring frequently with the wooden spoon, until the soup thickens, about 15 minutes. You should have about 2½ cups soup.

4 Using the pot holder, carefully remove the saucepan from the heat. Taste the soup with the table spoon (careful, it's hot) and add more salt or pepper, if you like. Ladle the soup into bowls or mugs and serve immediately with the crackers.

Makes 2 servings

EQUIPMENT

- ❑ **measuring cups & spoons**
- ❑ **cutting board**
- ❑ **sharp knife**
- ❑ **table spoon**
- ❑ **medium frying pan or griddle**
- ❑ **pot holder**
- ❑ **metal spatula**

crispy cheese quesadillas

INGREDIENTS

1 **avocado**

4 **flour tortillas, each 8 inches in diameter**

1 **cup shredded Monterey jack cheese**

1 **cup shredded extra-sharp cheddar cheese**

2 **tablespoons butter, cut into 4 equal pieces**

1 **recipe Fresh Tomato Salsa (page 53)**

1 Cut the avocado in half lengthwise. Twist the halves in opposite directions and lift away one half. Scoop out the pit with the spoon. Cut each half into slices and peel away the skin.

2 Lay the tortillas on the cutting board. Scatter one-fourth of the jack cheese and one-fourth of the cheddar cheese over one-half of each tortilla. Fold the uncovered half over the cheese and press gently to form a quesadilla.

3 Add 1 piece of the butter to the frying pan or griddle and set over medium heat. When the butter is melted, add 1 filled tortilla to the pan. Cook until the underside is golden brown, about 2 minutes. Holding the pan steady with the pot holder, use the spatula to turn the quesadilla over. Continue to cook, pressing gently on the quesadilla with the spatula, until the bottom is golden and the cheese is melted, about 2 minutes.

4 Using the spatula, transfer the quesadilla to the cutting board. Cut into 4 wedges with the sharp knife and place on a plate. Repeat step 3 with the remaining filled tortillas, adding 1 piece of the butter to the pan to cook each one. Cut each quesadilla into 4 wedges.

5 Serve with avocado slices and the salsa.

Makes 4 servings

use your favorite
melting cheeses

**use chopsticks and a spoon
to eat this Asian-flavored noodle soup**

EQUIPMENT

- ❑ measuring cups & spoons
- ❑ cutting board
- ❑ sharp knife
- ❑ medium saucepan with lid
- ❑ long-handled wooden spoon
- ❑ slotted spoon
- ❑ pot holder
- ❑ ladle

oodles of noodles⁕

INGREDIENTS

4 cups vegetable or chicken broth

2 ounces dried vermicelli

¾ cup fresh or frozen peas

½ cup diced firm tofu

1 tablespoon chopped fresh chives

1 teaspoon Asian sesame oil

1 Pour the vegetable or chicken broth into the medium saucepan, cover, and set over high heat. Bring the broth to a boil. When it boils, reduce the heat to medium.

2 Remove the lid. Add the vermicelli and peas. Simmer, uncovered, stirring frequently with the wooden spoon to keep the pasta from sticking together, for 5 minutes.

3 Add the tofu and continue to simmer until the noodles are al dente (tender but still firm to the bite) and the peas are tender, about 2 minutes longer. To test, using the slotted spoon, scoop out a few noodles and a few peas. Set them on the cutting board to cool for a few seconds. Taste them. If they are tender, they are done.

4 Using the pot holder, carefully remove the saucepan from the heat. Stir in the chives and sesame oil. Ladle into soup bowls and serve immediately.

Makes 2 servings

EQUIPMENT

- ❏ measuring spoons
- ❏ cutting board & sharp knife
- ❏ plate
- ❏ paper towels
- ❏ small frying pan

- ❏ table fork
- ❏ toaster
- ❏ table knife
- ❏ 4 sandwich picks

triple-decker turkey club

INGREDIENTS

2 slices bacon

3 slices whole-wheat bread

3 tablespoons mayonnaise

3 slices roasted turkey breast

salt and pepper

2 small green lettuce leaves

2 slices tomato

1 Line the plate with 2 paper towels. In the small frying pan, arrange the bacon slices flat and without overlapping. Set the pan over medium heat and cook the bacon until it is golden brown on the bottom, about 4 minutes. Using the table fork, turn the slices over. Be careful: The bacon can pop and the grease is very hot! Continue cooking until the bacon is golden brown on the second side, about 4 minutes longer. Turn off the heat. Using the fork, carefully lift the bacon slices from the pan and lay them on the paper towels. Ask an adult to help you discard the bacon grease.

2 Toast the bread until golden. Set the slices side by side on a work surface. Using the table knife, spread 1 tablespoon of the mayonnaise on top of each slice of toast.

3 Fold the turkey slices so they fit on 1 slice of the toast and lay them on it. Sprinkle with salt and pepper. Place a second slice of toast on top of the turkey, mayonnaise side up. Stack the lettuce leaves and tomato slices on the toast. Arrange the cooked bacon slices on the tomatoes in the shape of a cross. Sprinkle with salt and pepper and top with the remaining toast, mayonnaise side down. Press gently.

4 Put the 4 picks into the sandwich, placing them in the shape of a cross. Using the sharp knife, cut the stack into 4 triangles. The picks will hold the layers together. Serve immediately.

Makes 1 big serving

there are different ingredients
on each layer

serve at a picnic or barbecue

EQUIPMENT

❏ measuring cups & spoons
❏ cutting board & sharp knife
❏ vegetable peeler
❏ small mixing bowl
❏ wooden spoon

❏ large pot with lid
❏ box grater-shredder
❏ slotted spoon
❏ colander
❏ pot holders

creamy tortellini salad

INGREDIENTS

For the dressing:

3   ounces cream cheese, at room temperature

½   cup plain yogurt

1   tablespoon finely chopped fresh dill

1   tablespoon finely chopped fresh chives

1   small clove garlic, finely chopped

    salt and pepper

For the pasta:

3   quarts water

    salt

1   large carrot, peeled

9   ounces fresh cheese-filled tortellini (about 2 cups)

¼   pound green beans, ends trimmed and cut into 1-inch pieces

2   tablespoons milk

    pepper

1 Make the dressing: In the small mixing bowl, mix together with the wooden spoon the cream cheese, yogurt, dill, chives, and garlic until smooth. Season to taste with salt and pepper. Set the dressing aside.

2 Pour the water into the large pot and add 2 teaspoons salt. Cover, set the pot over high heat, and bring the water to a rolling boil.

3 Meanwhile, shred the carrot: Using the large holes on the box grater-shredder, rub the carrot over the holes in short strokes to form thin, short strips. Set the shredded carrot aside.

4 When the water is at a rolling boil, slowly and carefully add the tortellini. Be careful: The water and steam are very hot! Using the slotted spoon, stir the tortellini so that they don't stick together. Reduce the heat to medium-high and boil gently for 4 minutes, stirring occasionally.

5 Add the cut-up beans to the pot with the tortellini and continue to boil for 2 more minutes. Add the shredded carrot to the pot and continue to cook until the pasta is al dente (tender but still firm to the bite) and the vegetables are tender, about 1 minute longer.

6 Set the colander in the sink. Have the pot holders ready. Ask an adult to help you pour the contents of the pot into the colander. Rinse the pasta and vegetables with cold water and drain well.

7 Dump the drained pasta and vegetables into a serving bowl. Add the dressing and the 2 tablespoons milk. Gently toss the salad with the wooden spoon until well blended. Season with salt and pepper. Serve warm or chilled.

Makes 4 servings

EQUIPMENT

❏ **measuring cups & spoons**
❏ **cutting board**
❏ **vegetable peeler**
❏ **sharp knife**
❏ **table knife**

veggie wraps*

INGREDIENTS

2   **large flour tortillas, each 9 inches in diameter**

6   **tablespoons cream cheese, at room temperature**

½   **small cucumber, peeled and thinly sliced**

1   **tomato, thinly sliced**

1   **cup alfalfa sprouts**

    salt and pepper

1 Lay the tortillas on a work surface. Using the table knife, spread 3 tablespoons of the cream cheese over each tortilla.

2 Divide the cucumber slices in half and arrange one-half of the slices on top of the cheese on each tortilla. Press down gently. Divide the tomato slices in half and arrange them on top of the cucumber. Divide the alfalfa sprouts in half and sprinkle them over the tomato. Sprinkle with salt and pepper.

3 Working with 1 tortilla at a time, fold about 2 inches of the right edge over onto itself. Press gently. Fold over the same amount on the opposite edge. Again press gently. You will have 2 straight sides and 2 rounded ones. Beginning with the rounded side closest to you, roll up the layered tortilla and vegetables, holding the folded edges down with your fingers as you roll. Repeat with second tortilla.

4 Place the wraps, seam side down, on the cutting board and cut in half on the diagonal with the sharp knife. Serve immediately.

Makes 2 servings

✳ = super-easy recipe!

use flavored tortillas, if you like

snacks

✳ = super-easy recipe!

- ❏ measuring cups
- ❏ eight 5-ounce popsicle molds or paper cups
- ❏ table spoon
- ❏ aluminum foil
- ❏ 8 popsicle sticks

frozen fruit-and-yogurt pops*

INGREDIENTS

1 cup strawberry yogurt

1 cup orange juice

1½ cups raspberry juice

1 Set the molds or paper cups on a work surface. Spoon an equal amount of the yogurt into each mold or cup and press down with the spoon to fill the bottom evenly. Cover the molds. If using cups, cover each with a square of aluminum foil, pressing it firmly around the sides. Poke a popsicle stick through each foil cover, pushing it into the middle of the yogurt. Set the molds or cups in the freezer until beginning to set, about 40 minutes.

2 Remove the molds from the freezer. If using cups, carefully lift off the foil, but leave the sticks in place. Pour an equal amount of the orange juice into each mold or cup. Cover, return the molds or cups to the freezer, and freeze until firm, about 40 minutes. Repeat the procedure with the raspberry juice. Freeze until solid, about 4 hours or for as long as overnight.

3 To serve, slip the pops from the molds or remove the foil and peel away the paper cups.

Makes 8 pops

mix and match your favorite flavors

these make great after-school snacks

EQUIPMENT

❏ measuring cups & spoons   ❏ table fork
❏ 2 baking sheets   ❏ rubber spatula
❏ aluminum foil   ❏ oven mitts
❏ medium mixing bowl   ❏ 2 cooling racks

nutty jumbles

INGREDIENTS

1   **tablespoon soft butter for greasing baking sheets**

2   **egg whites**

½   **cup firmly packed light brown sugar**

1   **teaspoon vanilla extract**

    pinch of salt

1   **cup sliced almonds**

1   **cup chopped pecans**

1   **cup chopped walnuts**

1 Preheat the oven to 350°F. Line the 2 baking sheets with aluminum foil and lightly grease with the 1 tablespoon soft butter.

2 In the mixing bowl, combine the egg whites, brown sugar, vanilla, and salt. Stir with the table fork, mashing any lumps of sugar, until the mixture is frothy and smooth. Add the almonds, pecans, and walnuts. Mix with the fork until all the nuts are well coated, scraping down the sides of the bowl with the rubber spatula.

3 Drop heaping table-spoonfuls of the nut mixture onto the prepared baking sheets, spacing them about 2 inches apart. As you work, scrape down the sides of the bowl and stir the mixture occasionally. Flatten the mounds slightly. Place 1 baking sheet in the oven and bake until the nuts are well browned, 14 to 16 minutes. Using oven mitts, remove the baking sheet from the oven and set it on a rack to cool completely. Bake the second sheet of jumbles.

4 Using your fingers, carefully peel the cooled jumbles from the foil. Store in an airtight container at room temperature for up to 1 week.

Makes 24 cookies

- ❏ measuring cups & spoons
- ❏ box grater-shredder
- ❏ 9-inch glass pie dish
- ❏ mixing bowls
- ❏ table fork
- ❏ rubber spatula
- ❏ toothpick
- ❏ oven mitts
- ❏ cooling rack
- ❏ sharp knife

cheddar corn bread wedges

INGREDIENTS

1	teaspoon butter, at room temperature, for greasing pie dish
1½	cups all-purpose flour
½	cup cornmeal
¼	cup sugar
2½	teaspoons baking powder
¼	teaspoon salt
1	cup buttermilk
⅓	cup vegetable oil
1	egg
¾	cup shredded extra-sharp cheddar cheese

1 Preheat the oven to 375°F. Lightly grease the pie dish with the soft butter.

2 In a medium mixing bowl, combine the flour, cornmeal, sugar, baking powder, and salt. Stir with the table fork until well blended.

3 In another medium mixing bowl, combine the buttermilk, oil, and egg. Mix with the fork until well blended.

4 Pour the buttermilk mixture into the flour mixture. Gently stir with the rubber spatula until almost blended. Add the cheese and stir just until blended.

5 Using the rubber spatula, scrape the batter into the prepared pie dish. Bake until the corn bread is browned on top and the toothpick inserted into the center comes out clean, about 25 minutes. Using oven mitts, remove the pie dish from the oven and set it on the rack to cool.

6 Using the sharp knife, cut the corn bread into 12 wedges. Serve warm or at room temperature.

Makes 12 servings

pack a wedge in your lunch box or serve alongside creamy tomato soup

sweet, tart, and refreshing

EQUIPMENT

❏ measuring cups
❏ cutting board & sharp knife
❏ citrus juicer
❏ pitcher

❏ long-handled spoon
❏ small fine-mesh sieve
❏ small bowl
❏ small spoon

old-fashioned pink lemonade*

INGREDIENTS

2   large lemons

1½   cups water

⅓   cup sugar

2   large strawberries

     ice cubes (optional)

1 Cut the lemons in half across the middle. Using the citrus juicer, squeeze the juice from each half. You should have about ½ cup juice.

2 Pour the lemon juice into the pitcher. Add the water and sugar. Stir with the long-handled spoon until the sugar is dissolved.

3 On the cutting board, using the knife, cut off the green stems from the strawberries. Cut the strawberries in half.

4 Set the fine-mesh sieve over the small bowl. Put the strawberry halves in the sieve and mash with the back of the small spoon, pushing the berries through the sieve. Pour the strained strawberries into the lemonade. Make sure to scrape the underside of the sieve, adding what comes through to the juice. Throw away anything left inside the sieve. Stir the lemonade until well blended and pink. Cover and refrigerate until well chilled.

5 To serve, pour the lemonade into tall glasses. Or fill glasses with ice cubes and then pour in the lemonade.

Makes 2 servings

= super-easy recipe!

EQUIPMENT

- ❏ measuring cups & spoons
- ❏ medium saucepan
- ❏ wooden spoon
- ❏ pot holder
- ❏ medium bowl
- ❏ plastic wrap

the best rice pudding*

INGREDIENTS

3½ cups milk

½ cup long-grain white rice

¼ cup sugar

1½ teaspoons vanilla extract

pinch of salt

mixed fresh berries (optional)

1 Put the milk and rice in the saucepan and set it over high heat. Bring to a boil and reduce the heat to medium-low. Simmer, stirring frequently with the wooden spoon, until the mixture is very thick with mostly the rice and hardly any milk visible, 30 to 35 minutes. Remember to scrape down the sides of the pan regularly. Toward the end of the cooking, stir more frequently to prevent the mixture from sticking or scorching.

2 Using the pot holder, carefully remove the pan from the heat. Add the sugar, vanilla, and salt and stir until the sugar is dissolved.

3 Carefully pour the rice mixture into the medium bowl. Put a large piece of plastic wrap over the bowl, and press it directly onto the surface of the pudding. This prevents a skin from forming. Refrigerate until well chilled.

4 To serve, spoon the chilled pudding into glasses or bowls and sprinkle a few berries on top, if you like. Serve at once.

Makes 6 servings

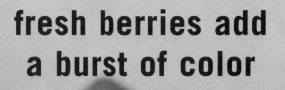

fresh berries add a burst of color

* = super-easy recipe!

good with crispy cheese
quesadillas, too

EQUIPMENT

- ❏ measuring cups & spoons
- ❏ cutting board
- ❏ small, sharp knife
- ❏ 2 small bowls
- ❏ medium mixing bowl
- ❏ wooden spoon
- ❏ plastic wrap

fresh tomato salsa

INGREDIENTS

1½ pounds (4 medium) ripe tomatoes

½ cup chopped green bell pepper

¼ cup chopped red onion

¼ cup lightly packed fresh cilantro leaves, chopped

1 small clove garlic, finely chopped

1 large lime

2 tablespoons olive oil

salt and black pepper

cayenne pepper (optional)

1 Place 1 tomato on the cutting board. With the tip of the small knife, cut out the stem end. Cut the tomato in half across the middle. Holding each tomato half over a small bowl, squeeze gently. Using your fingers, scoop out the seeds into the bowl. Then chop both halves. Scoop up all the juices on the cutting board with the diced tomatoes and put them into the medium mixing bowl. Repeat with the remaining tomatoes. Discard the seeds.

2 Add the bell pepper, red onion, cilantro, and garlic. Stir with the wooden spoon. Using the sharp knife, cut the lime in half across the middle. Squeeze the lime halves over a small bowl. Measure 3 tablespoons lime juice and add to the tomato mixture. Add the olive oil, ¼ teaspoon salt, a pinch of black pepper, and a pinch of cayenne pepper, if you want the salsa to be spicier. Stir gently. Taste and add more salt, black pepper, and cayenne pepper, if you like.

3 Serve immediately with Cheese-and-Spice Tortilla Chips (page 58) or, for better flavor, cover with plastic wrap and refrigerate for a few hours or for as long as 2 days.

Makes about 3 cups salsa

EQUIPMENT

- ❏ measuring cups
- ❏ cutting board & sharp knife
- ❏ 8-inch square baking dish
- ❏ small saucepan
- ❏ wooden spoon
- ❏ pot holder
- ❏ medium mixing bowl
- ❏ plastic wrap
- ❏ offset wide metal spatula (optional)

apple jiggles

INGREDIENTS

4   **cups apple juice**

2   **envelopes (¼ ounce each) unflavored gelatin**

2   **cups mixed fruits such as chopped strawberries, chopped peaches, whole blueberries, and halved seedless grapes**

1 Have ready the 8-inch square baking dish. Make room in the refrigerator for the mixing bowl.

2 Pour 1 cup of the apple juice into the small saucepan. Sprinkle the gelatin over the apple juice and let stand until the gelatin plumps up, about 2 minutes. Set the pan over medium-low heat and stir with the wooden spoon until the liquid is completely clear and the gelatin is dissolved, about 6 minutes. Using the pot holder, remove the pan from the heat and pour the liquid into the mixing bowl. Add the remaining 3 cups apple juice and stir until blended.

3 Set the bowl of apple juice and gelatin in the refrigerator. Chill, stirring every 5 minutes, until slightly thickened, about 1 hour.

4 When the mixture is the consistency of unbeaten egg whites, remove it from the refrigerator and gently stir in the mixed fruit. The fruit will be suspended in the gelatin.

Pour the mixture into the 8-inch baking dish, cover with plastic wrap, and refrigerate until firm, about 4 hours or for as long as overnight. Spoon into serving dishes or, using the offset spatula, cut into 9 squares and serve.

Makes 9 servings

**preparing homemade
gelatin is easy and fun**

**dip your favorite fruit, fresh or dried—
pretzels and cookies are good, too**

- ❏ cutting board & sharp knife
- ❏ 2 baking sheets
- ❏ aluminum foil
- ❏ pot holders
- ❏ small saucepan & small heatproof bowl
- ❏ wooden spoon
- ❏ rubber spatula

chocolate-dipped treats*

＊ = super-easy recipe!

INGREDIENTS

about 5 dried apricots

about 5 small pretzels

about 10 fresh cherries on stems

about 10 fresh strawberries with stems

about 5 dried pineapple rings, cut in half

about 5 graham crackers, broken into quarters

6 **ounces semisweet chocolate chips**

1 Line the 2 baking sheets with aluminum foil. Pile the dippers—apricots, pretzels, cherries, strawberries, pineapple, and graham crackers—next to the baking sheets and leave a space for the melted chocolate in between. Put down a pot holder for the chocolate pan or bowl—it will be hot!

2 Fill the small saucepan half full with water. Choose a small, deep heatproof bowl that fits snugly on the saucepan. Be sure the bottom of the bowl does not touch the water. Add the chocolate to the small bowl and set the whole thing (water-filled pan and bowl) over medium heat.

3 Heat the chocolate, stirring often with the wooden spoon, until it is melted, about 5 minutes. During that time, the water should simmer, not boil. Turn off the heat. Ask an adult to remove the bowl from the saucepan of water. Be careful: The steam is very hot! Set the bowl of chocolate on the pot holder next to the dippers.

4 Dunk a dipper into the chocolate to cover halfway. Let the excess chocolate drip back into the bowl. Place the dipper on a foil-lined baking sheet. Repeat with the remaining dippers, placing them on the baking sheets. Occasionally, give the bowl of chocolate a scrape with the rubber spatula. Reheat the chocolate if it cools down too much and hardens. Refrigerate any leftover chocolate in an airtight container.

5 Set the dippers in the refrigerator until the chocolate has set, about 15 minutes. Eat some now and save the rest in airtight containers. The dried fruit, pretzels, and grahams will keep for 1 week in a cool place. The fresh fruit will keep about 3 days in the fridge.

Makes a ton of snacks

- ❏ measuring cups & spoons
- ❏ baking sheet
- ❏ aluminum foil
- ❏ small saucepan
- ❏ wooden spoon
- ❏ pot holder
- ❏ mixing bowl & fork
- ❏ cutting board & sharp knife
- ❏ pastry brush
- ❏ metal spatula
- ❏ oven mitts
- ❏ cooling rack

cheese-and-spice tortilla chips*

INGREDIENTS

¼	cup (½ stick) butter, cut in half
⅓	cup grated Parmesan cheese
1	tablespoon sesame seeds
1	tablespoon poppy seeds
¼	teaspoon sweet paprika
	pinch of salt
	pinch of pepper
6	flour tortillas, each 6 inches in diameter

1 Preheat the oven to 400°F. Line the baking sheet with aluminum foil.

2 Put the butter in the small saucepan and set it over medium heat. Stir with the wooden spoon until the butter is melted, 1 to 2 minutes. Using the pot holder, remove the pan from the heat and set it aside to cool.

3 In a small mixing bowl, combine the cheese, sesame seeds, poppy seeds, paprika, salt, and pepper. Stir with the table fork until completely blended.

4 Lay the tortillas on the cutting board without letting them overlap. Using the pastry brush, brush the melted butter all over the top side of each tortilla. Using your fingers, sprinkle the cheese and spice mixture evenly over the tortillas, using about 1½ tablespoons on each. Gently spread and press the mixture onto the tortillas.

5 Using the sharp knife, cut each tortilla in half. Cut each half into 4 equal triangles. Move the triangles with your fingers or spatula to the prepared baking sheet and arrange close together.

6 Bake until the triangles are golden brown, about 8 minutes. Using oven mitts, remove the baking sheet from the oven and set it on the rack. Let the chips cool completely before eating. Store any leftovers in an airtight container at room temperature for up to 3 days.

Makes 4 dozen chips

dip these chips into fresh tomato salsa

✳ = super-easy recipe!

pack these bars in your
backpack for a midday treat

- ❏ measuring cups & spoons
- ❏ cutting board
- ❏ small, sharp knife
- ❏ small saucepan
- ❏ wooden spoon
- ❏ pot holder
- ❏ 9-inch square baking pan
- ❏ aluminum foil
- ❏ kitchen scissors
- ❏ medium mixing bowl
- ❏ oven mitts
- ❏ cooling rack
- ❏ ruler

apricot oatmeal bars

INGREDIENTS

¾	cup (1½ sticks) butter, cut up
2	teaspoons soft butter for greasing foil
1	cup firmly packed dried apricots
1½	cups old-fashioned rolled oats
1	cup all-purpose flour
1	cup firmly packed dark brown sugar
¼	teaspoon salt
¼	teaspoon ground cinnamon
1½	teaspoons vanilla extract

1 Put the ¾ cup butter in the small saucepan and set over medium-high heat. Stir with the wooden spoon until the butter is melted, about 2 minutes. Using the pot holder, remove the saucepan from the heat and set it aside to cool.

2 Preheat the oven to 350°F. Line the bottom and sides of the 9-inch square baking pan with a large piece of aluminum foil (some foil hanging over the edges is fine). Lightly grease the foil with the soft butter. Using the kitchen scissors, snip the apricots into about ½-inch pieces.

3 In the mixing bowl, combine the rolled oats, flour, brown sugar, salt, and cinnamon. Mix with the wooden spoon until well blended and no lumps of sugar remain.

4 Add the snipped apricots, melted butter, and vanilla to the bowl. Stir until well blended. The dough will be moist and crumbly. Dump the dough into the prepared baking pan. Press the dough into the pan with your fingers.

5 Bake until the top is golden brown, 35 to 40 minutes. Using the oven mitts, remove the pan from the oven and set on the rack to cool completely.

6 Lift the foil and the oatmeal bars from the pan and place on a work surface. Peel away the foil from the sides and bottom. Using the small, sharp knife, cut the big square into 1½-by-3-inch rectangles. Store in an airtight container.

Makes 18 bar cookies

look for the ripest fruits

- ❏ measuring cups & spoons
- ❏ cutting board
- ❏ small, sharp knife
- ❏ large mixing bowl
- ❏ small mixing bowl
- ❏ wooden spoon
- ❏ plastic wrap

rainbow fruit salad

INGREDIENTS

2	ripe plums
1	ripe nectarine or peach
2	cups (1 pint) strawberries
1	cup blueberries
1	cup raspberries
½	cored, peeled pineapple (store-bought)
1	orange
2	tablespoons sugar (optional)

1 Rinse and dry off the plums and nectarine or peach. Carefully rinse and dry off the berries.

2 On the cutting board, using the small, sharp knife, cut off the green stems from the strawberries. Cut the strawberries in half lengthwise and put them in the large mixing bowl. Cut each plum in half, remove the pit, and cut each half into wedges. Add to the bowl. Do the same to the nectarine or peach and add to the bowl along with the blueberries and the raspberries. Place the pineapple, flat side down, on the cutting board. Cut into 1-inch-thick slices. Cut each half circle into 4 chunks and add to the bowl.

3 Using the sharp knife, cut the orange across the middle. Hold each half over the small bowl and squeeze. Pick out any seeds and measure ¼ cup juice.

4 Sprinkle the fruits with the sugar, if using, and the ¼ cup juice. Gently toss the fruits with the wooden spoon until well mixed. Cover the bowl with plastic wrap and refrigerate for at least 1 hour to chill well.

5 When ready to serve, divide the fruit salad among serving bowls and spoon the juice over the top.

Makes 8 servings

✱ = super-easy recipe!

main courses & side dishes

* = super-easy recipe!

use your favorite pasta shape

- ❏ measuring cups & spoons
- ❏ box grater
- ❏ large saucepan with lid
- ❏ wooden spoon
- ❏ wire whisk
- ❏ pot holders
- ❏ large pot with lid
- ❏ long-handled wooden fork
- ❏ colander

macaroni and cheese

INGREDIENTS

2 tablespoons butter

2 tablespoons all-purpose flour

1⅔ cups milk

1 cup shredded extra-sharp cheddar cheese

2 tablespoons grated Parmesan cheese

4 quarts (16 cups) water

   salt

1 pound dried fusilli pasta

   pinch of pepper

1 Put the butter in the large saucepan and set the pan over medium heat. Stir with the wooden spoon until the butter is melted, about 2 minutes. Add the flour and whisk it together with the butter until smooth and bubbly but not browned, about 2 minutes. If the mixture begins to brown, reduce the heat to medium-low. With the pan still on the heat, slowly pour in the milk, whisking constantly. Cook, continuing to whisk, until the mixture is smooth, thickened, and gently boiling, 5 to 7 minutes.

2 Using a pot holder, remove the pan from the heat and add the cheddar and Parmesan cheeses. Whisk until the cheeses melt and the sauce is smooth. Cover with the lid and set aside.

3 Put the water in the large pot and add 1 tablespoon salt. Set the pot over high heat, cover with the lid, and bring to a rolling boil. Remove the lid. Be careful: The steam is very hot! Slowly and carefully add the pasta, then stir it with the long-handled wooden fork. Boil the pasta, uncovered, until al dente (tender but still firm to the bite), about 8 minutes, or according to package directions. Stir occasionally to prevent from sticking.

4 Set the colander in the sink. Have the pot holders ready. When the pasta is cooked, ask an adult to pour the contents of the pot into the colander. Let the pasta drain completely, shaking the colander a few times. Add the drained pasta, ¼ teaspoon salt, and the pepper to the cheese sauce. Stir until well blended. Serve immediately.

Makes 4 servings

EQUIPMENT

- ❑ measuring cups & spoons
- ❑ large colander
- ❑ paper towels or salad spinner
- ❑ salad bowl & small mixing bowl
- ❑ small wire whisk
- ❑ plastic wrap
- ❑ salad tongs or 2 large spoons

green salad with vinaigrette*

INGREDIENTS

½   **pound butter lettuce or mixed salad greens, torn into small pieces (about 8 cups)**

2   **tablespoons red wine vinegar**

1½   **teaspoons Dijon mustard**

1   **teaspoon fresh thyme leaves, optional**

⅛   **teaspoon salt**

     pinch of pepper

6   **tablespoons olive oil**

1 Put the torn salad greens in the colander and gently rinse well under cold, running water. Drain well and dry between layers of paper towels or spin dry in a salad spinner. Pile the dry greens in a salad bowl and cover loosely with a damp paper towel. Refrigerate until ready to serve.

2 In a small mixing bowl, combine the vinegar, mustard, fresh thyme leaves, if using, salt, and pepper. Using the small whisk, stir until well blended. Whisking constantly, add the oil in a slow, steady stream until completely mixed. Taste the dressing and add more salt and pepper, if you like. Cover the bowl with plastic wrap and refrigerate until serving.

3 Just before serving, add about half of the dressing to the salad greens. Using salad tongs or large spoons, toss the greens until they are evenly coated with the dressing. Taste and add more dressing, if you like. Serve immediately.

Makes 6 servings

vinaigrette is a classic French dressing

here's a dish the whole family will love—
pork chops and apples taste great together

- ❏ measuring spoons
- ❏ cutting board
- ❏ sharp knife
- ❏ 8-inch square baking dish
- ❏ aluminum foil
- ❏ oven mitts
- ❏ table fork
- ❏ serving spoon

baked pork chops with apples

INGREDIENTS

4	red-skinned apples
1	tablespoon sugar
	pinch of ground cinnamon
4	boneless pork chops, each about ¾ inch thick
	salt and pepper
2	tablespoons butter, cut into small pieces

1 Preheat the oven to 375°F. Have ready the 8-inch square baking dish.

2 Set 1 apple on the cutting board and cut it in half lengthwise with the sharp knife. Cut each half in half again to make quarters. Place each quarter on its side and cut away the core. Cut each quarter lengthwise into ½-inch-thick slices. Repeat with the other apples. Pile the slices into the baking dish.

3 Sprinkle the sugar and cinnamon evenly over the apples.

4 Generously sprinkle both sides of the pork chops with salt and pepper. Tuck the chops into the pile of apples, rearranging the slices around them. Scatter the butter pieces over the tops of the pork chops and apple slices. Cover the baking dish with aluminum foil.

5 Bake for 40 minutes. Ask an adult to help you remove the foil from the baking dish. Be careful: The steam is very hot! Continue to cook until the pork chops are lightly browned and the apples are tender, about 20 minutes longer. Using oven mitts, remove the baking dish from the oven.

6 To serve, use the table fork to transfer each chop to a serving plate. Scoop up the apple slices and the juices with the serving spoon and place them around the chops.

Makes 4 servings

EQUIPMENT

- ❏ measuring cups & spoons
- ❏ cutting board
- ❏ sharp knife
- ❏ small saucepan with lid
- ❏ pot holder
- ❏ wooden spoon
- ❏ box grater-shredder
- ❏ citrus juicer
- ❏ medium mixing bowl
- ❏ table fork

couscous salad

INGREDIENTS

1¼ cups water

1   cup instant couscous

2   green onions

1   lemon, rinsed and dried

3   tablespoons olive oil

2   tablespoons finely chopped fresh parsley

     salt and pepper

12   cherry tomatoes, stems removed and cut in half

1 Pour the water into the small saucepan and set it over high heat. Bring the water to a boil. Once the water is boiling, using the pot holder, carefully remove the pan from the heat. Add the couscous and stir once with the wooden spoon. Cover the pan with the lid and set it aside until the water is absorbed, about 10 minutes.

2 Put the green onions on the cutting board and cut off the root ends with the sharp knife. Peel away the outer layer of skin. Cut the white part and about 2 inches of the green into thin slices and set aside. Using the small holes on the box grater, rub the lemon down over the holes in quick, short strokes. Grate only the yellow zest. Measure ½ teaspoon of the zest and set aside. Cut the lemon in half across the middle. Using the citrus juicer, squeeze the juice from each half. Measure ¼ cup of the juice and set aside.

3 Spoon the couscous into the mixing bowl and stir with the table fork to break apart any clumps. Add the lemon zest and juice, olive oil, parsley, 1 teaspoon salt, and a pinch of pepper. Using the table fork, stir until well blended. Add the cherry tomato halves and the sliced green onions. Gently stir until blended. Taste and add more salt and pepper, if you like.

4 Serve immediately, or cover with plastic wrap and refrigerate for up to 1 day.

Makes 6 servings

serve this salad alongside
deluxe turkey burgers

EQUIPMENT

- ❏ measuring cups & spoons
- ❏ large mixing bowl
- ❏ wooden spoon
- ❏ instant-read thermometer
- ❏ plastic wrap
- ❏ 2 baking sheets
- ❏ aluminum foil
- ❏ cutting board & plate
- ❏ sharp knife
- ❏ box grater-shredder
- ❏ ruler
- ❏ oven mitts

cheese and tomato pizza

INGREDIENTS

For the dough:

3   cups flour

1   package (¼ ounce) quick-rise yeast

2½ teaspoons salt

2   teaspoons sugar

1   cup warm water (115°F to 125°F)

2   tablespoons plus 1 teaspoon olive oil

For the topping:

4   ripe tomatoes

¾   pound mozzarella cheese

2   tablespoons olive oil

    salt and pepper

1 First, make the dough: Set aside ½ cup of the flour. In the large mixing bowl, combine the remaining 2½ cups flour, the yeast, salt, and sugar. Using the wooden spoon, stir until well blended.

2 Ask an adult to help you use the instant-read thermometer to check the temperature of the water. Add the water and 2 tablespoons olive oil to the flour mixture and stir with the wooden spoon until a rough dough forms. Dust a work surface with some of the reserved ½ cup flour. Dump the dough onto the surface.

3 Knead the dough, flouring your hands and the surface as needed: First, gather the dough together. Next, using the heel of one hand, push the top part of the dough away from you. Fold that piece over the dough nearest to you. Give the dough a quarter turn clockwise and repeat. Keep on kneading until the dough is smooth and no longer sticky, about 10 minutes. Gather the dough into a ball.

4 Wipe out the mixing bowl and grease it lightly with 1 teaspoon olive oil. Put the dough into the bowl and cover the bowl tightly with plastic wrap. Set the bowl in a warm spot and let the dough rise until doubled in bulk, about 45 minutes.

RECIPE CONTINUES

**making pizza from scratch
is easy and fun**

cheese and tomato pizza
CONTINUED

5 Adjust the oven rack to the lowest position. Preheat the oven to 425°F. Line the 2 baking sheets with the aluminum foil.

6 Prepare the toppings: Place 1 tomato on the cutting board. With the tip of the sharp knife, cut out the stem end. Cut the tomato across into thin slices. Repeat with the other 3 tomatoes.

7 Hold the box grater-shredder on the plate with one hand. With your other hand, move the mozzarella cheese up and down the large round holes to cut shreds. Keep your fingers away from the holes of the grater!

8 Lightly dust the work surface with some of the reserved flour. Dump out the risen dough onto the work surface and divide the dough in half using the knife.

9 Using your hands, shape one-half of the dough into a 9-by-13-inch rectangle. Transfer the rectangle to 1 foil-lined baking sheet (reshape it if necessary).

10 Drizzle the rectangle with 1 tablespoon of the olive oil and arrange half of the tomato slices on top. Sprinkle with half of the cheese and season with salt and pepper.

11 Bake the first pizza until the cheese is bubbling and the crust is browned, about 20 minutes. While the first pizza is baking, make a second pizza on the other foil-lined baking sheet with the remaining dough and toppings.

12 Using oven mitts, remove the first pizza from the oven. Slip the second pizza into the oven. Slide the baked pizza onto the cutting board. Using a sharp knife, cut the pizza into rectangles. Serve the pizzas piping hot.

Makes 4 to 6 servings

fresh tomato sauce

you can use this tomato sauce instead of fresh tomatoes on the pizza–it's good on pasta, too

❑ **measuring cups & spoons**
❑ **cutting board**
❑ **sharp knife**
❑ **medium bowl**
❑ **large frying pan**
❑ **wooden spoon**
❑ **pot holders**

INGREDIENTS

6 **large, ripe tomatoes**

¼ **cup olive oil**

1 **large onion, chopped**

2 **cloves garlic, finely chopped**

8 **fresh basil leaves, chopped**

salt and pepper

1 Place 1 tomato on the cutting board. With the tip of the sharp knife, cut out the stem end. Cut the tomato in half across the middle. Holding each tomato half over the medium bowl, squeeze gently. Using your fingers, scoop out the seeds into the bowl. Discard the seeds. Repeat with the other tomatoes. Coarsely chop the tomatoes and pile them into the same bowl. Set aside.

2 Pour the olive oil into the frying pan and set over medium heat. Add the chopped onions. Cook, stirring frequently with the wooden spoon, until the onions are soft, about 8 minutes. Add the garlic and cook, stirring, for 1 more minute.

3 Add the chopped tomatoes and any juices in the bowl to the frying pan. Simmer the sauce vigorously over medium heat, stirring frequently, until it has reduced and thickened, about 20 minutes. The tomato pieces will be soft but will still hold their shape.

4 Using the pot holders, carefully remove the pan from the heat. Ask an adult for help if it is too heavy. Stir in the basil, 1½ teaspoons salt, and ¼ teaspoon pepper. Taste and add more salt and pepper, if you like. Spoon the sauce over pizza dough or serve on top of cooked pasta. The sauce can be cooled, covered, and refrigerated for up to 3 days.

Makes about 3 cups sauce

EQUIPMENT

- ❏ measuring cups & spoons
- ❏ cutting board
- ❏ sharp knife
- ❏ medium frying pan
- ❏ wooden spoon
- ❏ pot holder

corn off the cob*

INGREDIENTS

4   **ears of corn**

¼   **cup (½ stick) butter**

    salt and pepper

1 Peel away the husk and silky threads from each ear of corn. Using both hands, snap the ears in half. Ask an adult to help if necessary.

2 Place half an ear, snapped end down, on the cutting board. Hold the top so it stays upright. Starting at the top, run the knife down the length of the corn, cutting between the cob and the kernels. Rotate the cob about one-quarter turn and cut again. Repeat until the cob is completely stripped of kernels. Repeat with the other corn halves.

3 Put the butter in the frying pan and set it over medium heat. When the butter is melted and foamy, stir in the corn kernels, ¼ teaspoon salt, and a pinch of pepper. Cook, stirring frequently with the wooden spoon, until the corn is bright yellow and crisp-tender, 3 to 5 minutes. Taste and add more salt and pepper, if you like. Using the pot holder, remove the pan from the heat and serve the corn immediately.

Makes 4 servings

corn is just as sweet
on or off the cob

cracker crumbs give this dish a crispy crunch

EQUIPMENT

- ❏ measuring cups & spoons
- ❏ small jelly-roll pan
- ❏ aluminum foil
- ❏ lock-top plastic bag
- ❏ rolling pin
- ❏ bowls
- ❏ table fork & knife
- ❏ paper towels
- ❏ oven mitts
- ❏ small, sharp knife

crunchy coated chicken breasts

INGREDIENTS

17   **Saltine crackers**

¼   **cup grated Parmesan cheese**

½   **teaspoon dried thyme**

     salt and pepper

2   **tablespoons olive oil**

4   **boneless, skinless chicken breast halves, about 6 ounces each**

2   **tablespoons Dijon mustard**

1 Preheat the oven to 425°F. Line the jelly-roll pan with aluminum foil and set it aside.

2 Put the crackers in the plastic bag. Press down on the bag to release the air and seal the top. Using the rolling pin, crush the crackers to make coarse crumbs.

3 Empty the crumbs into a shallow bowl. Add the Parmesan cheese, dried thyme, and a good pinch each of salt and pepper. Stir with the table fork until well mixed. Drizzle the olive oil over the crumbs and toss with the fork until the crumbs are evenly moistened.

4 Rinse the chicken breasts with cold water and pat dry with paper towels. Place them, skinned side up, on a work surface. Spoon the mustard into a small bowl. Using the table knife, spread the mustard over the top of each chicken breast. Sprinkle with salt and pepper.

5 Press the mustard-coated side of a chicken breast half into the crumb mixture. Place the chicken, crumb side up, on the foil-lined jelly-roll pan. Repeat with the other chicken breasts. Sprinkle any leftover crumbs on top of the breasts and pat them onto the chicken with your fingers.

6 Bake until the chicken is no longer pink in the middle when cut into with the sharp knife, about 25 minutes. Using oven mitts, remove the pan from the oven and serve the chicken immediately.

Makes 4 servings

- ❏ measuring spoons
- ❏ jelly-roll pan
- ❏ aluminum foil
- ❏ cutting board
- ❏ large, sharp knife
- ❏ vegetable peeler
- ❏ medium mixing bowl
- ❏ rubber spatula
- ❏ oven mitts

oven-baked carrot fries*

INGREDIENTS

1½ **pounds carrots
(10 medium)**

2 **tablespoons olive oil**

2 **teaspoons finely
chopped fresh
rosemary**

1 **teaspoon sugar**

½ **teaspoon salt**

pinch of pepper

1 Preheat the oven to 425°F. Line the jelly-roll pan with aluminum foil.

2 Using the sharp knife and cutting board, cut away the tip and end of each carrot. Place 1 carrot on the board and hold with one hand. Holding the peeler in the other hand, run it over the carrot, always peeling away from you. Turn the carrot as needed to peel completely. Repeat with the other carrots. Using the sharp knife, cut 1 carrot in half crosswise. Next, cut each half in half lengthwise. Finally, cut each half in half lengthwise again. You will end up with 8 sticks from the carrot. Repeat with the other carrots.

3 In the mixing bowl, combine the carrot sticks, olive oil, rosemary, sugar, salt, and pepper. Stir with the rubber spatula until the carrot sticks are evenly coated with all the other ingredients.

4 Dump the carrots onto the foil-lined jelly-roll pan, scraping out any herbs clinging to the sides of the bowl. Spread the sticks out as much as possible. Bake until the carrots are tender and well browned, about 20 minutes. Using oven mitts, remove the pan from the oven. Serve the carrot fries hot or at room temperature.

Makes 4 servings

carrots get sweet and tender
when oven baked

* = super-easy recipe!

here's how to build
a better burger

EQUIPMENT

❏ measuring cups & spoons
❏ medium mixing bowl
❏ table fork
❏ ruler
❏ plate

❏ large frying pan
❏ metal spatula
❏ pot holder
❏ small, sharp knife

deluxe turkey burgers

INGREDIENTS

½   cup seasoned dried bread crumbs

⅓   cup milk

3   tablespoons ketchup

1   egg

½   teaspoon salt

¼   teaspoon pepper

1   pound ground turkey

2   tablespoons vegetable oil

4   large sesame-seed buns

small lettuce leaves

ketchup and pickles

thin slices of tomato and red onion (optional)

1 In the medium mixing bowl, combine the bread crumbs and milk. Stir with the table fork until blended. Add the ketchup, egg, salt, and pepper. Stir until well blended. Add the ground turkey. Using the table fork, gently mix the ingredients together until just blended. Don't overwork the mixture, or your burgers will be tough.

2 Divide the mixture into 4 equal mounds. Lightly wet your hands with water and shape each mound into a flat circle about 4 inches in diameter. Place the burgers on the plate.

3 Add the vegetable oil to the frying pan and set over medium-low heat. Heat 1 minute and then tilt the pan to coat the bottom evenly with the oil. Using the metal spatula, place the burgers in the pan. Cook the burgers until the bottoms are browned, about 5 minutes. Holding the pan steady with the pot holder, use the spatula to flip the burgers. Continue cooking until the burgers are cooked through (no longer pink in the center), 5 to 7 minutes longer. To test, use the small knife and cut into the center of a burger. Using the pot holder, carefully remove the pan from the heat.

4 Lift the burgers from the pan with the spatula. Serve immediately on sesame-seed buns with lettuce leaves, ketchup, and pickles and with slices of tomato and red onion, if you like.

Makes 4 servings

- ❏ measuring cups & spoons
- ❏ large pot with lid
- ❏ long-handled fork
- ❏ medium saucepan
- ❏ 2 long-handled wooden spoons
- ❏ pot holders
- ❏ colander
- ❏ table fork

fettuccine alfredo*

INGREDIENTS

- 6 quarts (24 cups) water
- salt
- 1 pound dried fettuccine pasta
- 2 cups heavy cream
- 1 cup grated Parmesan cheese, plus more for sprinkling on top
- pepper
- pinch of ground nutmeg

1 Pour the water into the large pot and add 1 tablespoon salt. Set the pot over high heat, cover with the lid, and bring the water to a rolling boil. Remove the lid—careful of the steam! Slowly and carefully add the pasta, then stir it with the long-handled fork. Boil the pasta, uncovered, until al dente (tender but still firm to the bite), about 9 minutes, or according to package directions. Stir occasionally to prevent from sticking.

2 While the pasta is boiling, pour the cream into the medium saucepan. Set the pan over high heat and bring the cream to a boil. Reduce the heat to medium and simmer vigorously, stirring occasionally with a wooden spoon, until slightly thickened, about 5 minutes. Using a pot holder, remove the pan from the heat. Set the pan aside until the pasta is ready.

3 Set the colander in the sink. Have the pot holders ready. When the pasta is cooked, ask an adult to pour the contents of the pot into the colander. Drain quickly, shaking the colander, and dump the pasta back into the pot.

4 Add the warm cream to the pasta. Add the Parmesan cheese, ½ teaspoon salt, ½ teaspoon pepper, and nutmeg. Using the wooden spoons, toss until the ingredients are well blended. Taste with the table fork to see if you need more salt and pepper. Let sit 3 minutes for the pasta to absorb some of the sauce.

5 Spoon the pasta onto 4 serving plates and pour over any cream sauce remaining in the pot. Serve immediately with more grated Parmesan for sprinkling on top.

Makes 4 servings

buon appetito

an all-time favorite side dish

- ❏ measuring cups & spoons
- ❏ vegetable brush
- ❏ large saucepan
- ❏ small, sharp knife
- ❏ colander
- ❏ pot holders
- ❏ potato masher
- ❏ large spoon

smashed potatoes*

INGREDIENTS

1½ **pounds red-skinned potatoes (about 9 small potatoes)**

salt

¼ **cup (½ stick) butter, cut into 3 equal chunks**

½ **cup half-and-half or milk**

pinch of pepper

1 With the vegetable brush, scrub the potatoes clean under cold running water, but do not peel them. Put the potatoes in the large saucepan and add water to cover them by at least 1 inch. Add 2 teaspoons salt. Set the pan over high heat and bring the water to a boil. Reduce the heat to medium and simmer the potatoes until they are tender, 20 to 25 minutes. Poke a potato with the point of the small, sharp knife. The knife should glide easily through the potato.

2 Set the colander in the sink. Have the pot holders ready. When the potatoes are cooked, ask an adult to pour the contents of the saucepan into the colander. Shake the colander 2 or 3 times to get rid of any excess water. Put the drained potatoes back into the saucepan.

3 With the potato masher, press down on each potato until smashed. Add the butter, half-and-half or milk, ¼ teaspoon salt, and pepper. Continue to mash and stir the potatoes until they are almost smooth. Only small chunks should remain. Taste the potatoes and add more salt and pepper, if desired. Use the large spoon to scoop the

potatoes into a serving bowl and serve immediately.

Makes 4 servings

* = super-easy recipe!

EQUIPMENT

- ❑ measuring spoons
- ❑ cutting board & sharp knife
- ❑ medium mixing bowl
- ❑ wooden spoon
- ❑ wok or large frying pan
- ❑ 2 metal spatulas or 2 wooden spoons
- ❑ pot holders

super shrimp stir-fry

INGREDIENTS

- 1 **pound large, peeled and deveined shrimp**
- 3 **tablespoons soy sauce**
- 1 **clove garlic, finely chopped**
- 2 **tablespoons vegetable oil**
- 1 **small red bell pepper, coarsely chopped**
- 1 **small onion, coarsely chopped**
- 16 **snow peas, ends trimmed**
- 2 **tablespoons water**
- **pinch of pepper**

1 In the medium mixing bowl, combine the shrimp, 2 tablespoons of the soy sauce, and the garlic. Stir with the wooden spoon until the shrimp are evenly coated. Set aside for 10 minutes.

2 Add the vegetable oil to the wok or frying pan and set over medium-high heat. When the oil is hot (flick a drop of water into it; it should sputter), add the red pepper and onion. Cook, stirring constantly with the 2 spatulas or spoons, until the pepper is slightly softened, about 3 minutes. Add the snow peas and the shrimp mixture. Continue stirring and cooking until the shrimp turn pink and are cooked through, and the snow peas are tender but still crisp, about 3 minutes more.

3 Using the pot holders, carefully remove the wok or frying pan from the heat. Add the remaining 1 tablespoon soy sauce, the water, and the pepper. Stir until blended. Carefully transfer to a serving dish and serve immediately.

Makes 4 servings

**cook a pot of steamed rice
to serve with this dish**

desserts

✳ = super-easy recipe!

use your favorite
ice-cream flavor

- ❏ measuring cups & spoons
- ❏ 9-by-13-inch baking pan
- ❏ aluminum foil
- ❏ large saucepan
- ❏ wire whisk & pot holder
- ❏ rubber spatula
- ❏ toothpick & oven mitts
- ❏ cooling rack
- ❏ cutting board & sharp knife
- ❏ plastic wrap

homemade ice-cream sandwiches

INGREDIENTS

1 tablespoon butter, at room temperature, for greasing foil

¾ cup (1½ sticks) butter

¾ cup unsweetened cocoa powder

1½ cups sugar

3 eggs

2 teaspoons vanilla extract

1½ cups all-purpose flour

pinch of salt

1 quart (4 cups) chocolate chip ice cream, softened

1 Preheat the oven to 350°F. Line the bottom and sides of the 9-by-13-inch pan with aluminum foil (some foil hanging over the edges is fine). Lightly grease the foil with butter.

2 Put the ¾ cup butter into the saucepan and set it over medium heat. Stir with the whisk just until the butter is melted. Using the pot holder, remove the saucepan from the heat and add the cocoa powder. Whisk until the mixture is smooth and no lumps remain. Add the sugar and continue whisking until well blended. Let the mixture cool for 2 minutes.

3 Add the eggs and vanilla and whisk until well blended. Add the flour and salt. Using the rubber spatula, stir until the batter is blended. Scrape down the sides of the saucepan as needed.

4 Scrape the batter into the prepared baking pan and spread evenly. Bake until a toothpick inserted into the center comes out clean, about 20 minutes. Using oven mitts, remove the pan from the oven and set it on the rack. Let cool completely.

5 Using the ends of the foil, lift the brownie from the pan and set it on the cutting board. Cut the brownie in half lengthwise. Carefully loosen both halves from the foil. Using the rubber spatula, spread the softened ice cream evenly over one half of the brownie into a layer about 1 inch thick. Top with the other half of the brownie and press down gently. Wrap in the foil. Freeze until hard, about 6 hours.

6 Peel away the foil and cut into 8 to 10 sandwiches. Serve immediately. You can also wrap the sandwiches in plastic wrap and store them in the freezer for up to 2 weeks.

Makes 8 to 10 sandwiches

EQUIPMENT

❑ measuring cups & spoons
❑ cutting board & sharp knife
❑ large mixing bowl
❑ electric mixer
❑ rubber spatula

❑ plastic wrap & ruler
❑ 3 baking sheets
❑ aluminum foil
❑ oven mitts
❑ cooling racks

buttery pecan cookies*

INGREDIENTS

1   cup (2 sticks) butter, at room temperature

⅔   cup sugar

     pinch of salt

1   teaspoon vanilla extract

2   cups all-purpose flour

½   cup chopped pecans

1 In the large mixing bowl, combine the butter, sugar, salt, and vanilla. Using the electric mixer set on medium speed, beat the mixture until it is smooth. Turn off the mixer a few times so you can scrape down the sides of the bowl with the rubber spatula. Add the flour and nuts. Continue mixing until the dough looks like moist pebbles, then turn off the mixer.

2 Gently squeeze the dough together with your hands. When the dough comes together in a mass, place it on a large piece of plastic wrap. Using your hands, shape it into a log 10 inches long and about 2 inches in diameter. Wrap the log in the plastic wrap and refrigerate until firm, about 3 hours.

3 Preheat the oven to 350°F. Line the 3 baking sheets with aluminum foil.

4 Unwrap the dough and place it on the cutting board. Using the knife, cut the log into slices ¼ inch thick. Arrange the slices about 1 inch apart on the foil-lined baking sheets. Place 1 baking sheet in the oven and bake the cookies until their edges are golden brown, 14 to 16 minutes. Using oven mitts, remove the baking sheet from the oven and set on a rack to cool completely. Repeat with the second and then the third baking sheets.

5 Lift the cooled cookies off the baking sheets with your fingers. Store the cookies in an airtight container.

Makes about 40 cookies

roll the dough into a log, slice it, and bake—it's easy

the original
chocolate pudding

EQUIPMENT

❏ measuring cups
❏ small saucepan & small heatproof bowl
❏ wooden spoon

❏ large mixing bowl
❏ electric mixer
❏ rubber spatula
❏ plastic wrap

chocolate mousse*

INGREDIENTS

1¼ cups semisweet chocolate chips, or 8 ounces semisweet chocolate, chopped

2 cups heavy cream, well chilled

1 Fill the small saucepan half full with water. Choose a small, deep heatproof bowl that fits snugly on the saucepan. Be sure the bottom of the bowl does not touch the water. Add the chocolate to the small bowl and set the whole thing (water-filled pan and bowl) over medium heat.

2 Heat the chocolate, stirring often with the wooden spoon, until it is melted, about 5 minutes. During that time, the water should simmer, not boil. Adjust the heat up or down as necessary.

3 Turn off the heat. Ask an adult to remove the bowl from the saucepan of water. Set the bowl aside to cool slightly.

4 Pour the cream into the large mixing bowl. Using the electric mixer set on medium speed, beat the cream until slightly thickened, about 30 seconds. Add the warm chocolate to the cream. Continue beating on medium speed, scraping down the sides of the bowl with the rubber spatula, until soft peaks form, about 1 minute. To test, turn off the mixer and lift the beaters. If the cream makes soft little peaks that flop over slightly, it is ready.

5 Spoon the mousse into serving cups or glasses. Cover with plastic wrap and refrigerate for at least 2 hours before serving.

Makes 8 servings

super-easy recipe!

EQUIPMENT

- ❏ measuring cups & spoons
- ❏ cutting board
- ❏ sharp knife
- ❏ lock-top plastic bag
- ❏ rolling pin
- ❏ 6 tall serving glasses
- ❏ large table spoon
- ❏ plastic wrap

apricot-ginger parfaits

INGREDIENTS

½ **recipe Sweetened Whipped Cream (page 105)**

6 **ripe apricots**

20 **crisp gingersnaps**

For serving:

1 **ripe apricot**

6 **fresh mint sprigs**

1 Make the Sweetened Whipped Cream. Cut each of the 6 apricots in half and pull out the pit. Cut each half into slices about ½ inch thick. Divide the slices into 12 equal piles.

2 Put the gingersnaps into the plastic bag. Push out the air and seal the bag. Using the rolling pin, crush the cookies to make coarse crumbs. The pieces should be the size of peas and no larger. You should have about 1½ cups crumbs.

3 Set the serving glasses on a work surface. Sprinkle about 1 heaping tablespoon of the gingersnap crumbs into the bottom of each glass. Spoon about 1 heaping tablespoon of the whipped cream over the crumbs. Place 1 pile of apricots on top of the cream. Repeat with the remaining ingredients, ending with whipped cream. You will have 3 layers of crumbs, 3 layers of cream, and 2 layers of fruit in each glass.

4 Cover the glasses with plastic wrap and refrigerate for at least 2 hours. The longer the parfaits are refrigerated, the softer the crumbs will become.

5 Just before serving, cut the remaining apricot in half and pull out the pit. Cut each half into 3 slices. Top each parfait with an apricot slice and a mint sprig.

Makes 6 servings

a parfait is a layered
fruit and cream dessert

- ❏ measuring cups & spoons
- ❏ 2 large mixing bowls
- ❏ wooden spoon
- ❏ pastry blender or
  2 table knives
- ❏ plastic wrap
- ❏ cutting board
- ❏ vegetable peeler
- ❏ sharp knife
- ❏ 9-inch pie dish
- ❏ baking sheet
- ❏ rolling pin
- ❏ ruler
- ❏ long metal spatula
- ❏ scissors
- ❏ oven mitts
- ❏ cooling rack

all-american apple pie

INGREDIENTS

For the pie dough:

3½ cups all-purpose flour

2 tablespoons
granulated sugar

½ teaspoon salt

¾ cup (1½ sticks) very
cold butter, cut into
½-inch pieces

½ cup very cold water

For the apple filling:

6 large tart apples,
about 2¾ pounds

½ cup firmly packed
light brown sugar

2 tablespoons
all-purpose flour

1 teaspoon ground
cinnamon

1 teaspoon vanilla
extract

1 First, make the pie dough: In a large mixing bowl, combine 2½ cups of the flour, the granulated sugar, and the salt. Using the wooden spoon, stir until well blended.

2 Drop the butter pieces into the flour mixture. Using the pastry blender or the table knives, work the butter and flour together with a quick chopping motion. If using 2 knives, cut in by drawing the knives in opposite directions through the butter and flour mixture. Scrape off the excess butter that clings to the pastry blender or knives. Keep cutting in the butter until the mixture looks like coarse crumbs with only very small pieces of butter still visible.

3 Pour the cold water over the top of the flour-butter mixture. Using the wooden spoon, stir gently until the mixture forms moist crumbs. Dump the crumbs onto a work surface. Divide into 2 equal piles. Using your hands, press each pile of crumbs into a flat disk. Wrap the disks separately in plastic wrap and refrigerate until well chilled, for at least 30 minutes or for as long as 2 days.

4 Make the apple filling: Holding 1 apple steady on the cutting board, peel the apple with the vegetable peeler. Set the apple on the board and cut it in half lengthwise with the sharp knife. Cut each half in half again to make quarters. Place each quarter on its side and cut away the core. Cut each quarter lengthwise into ½-inch-thick slices. Repeat with the other apples. Pile the slices into the other large mixing bowl. Add the brown sugar, flour, cinnamon, and vanilla. Using the wooden spoon, stir until well blended.

RECIPE CONTINUES

serve this classic American dessert with a dollop of whipped cream

5 To assemble and bake the pie, remove the dough from the refrigerator. Set the 9-inch pie dish on the baking sheet. Preheat the oven to 425°F.

6 Sprinkle the work surface with a little of the remaining 1 cup flour and set the rest aside. Unwrap 1 disk of dough and set it in the middle of the floured surface. Using the rolling pin, press gently on the disk to flatten slightly.

7 Sprinkle the top of the dough with a little more of the flour. Place the rolling pin on the center of the dough. Using a little pressure, roll the pin over the dough to the far outer edge. Give the dough a little turn to the right, sprinkle with a little more of the flour, and, starting from the center, roll again. Repeat the turning, flouring, and rolling until you have a large round circle about 14 inches in diameter. If the dough begins to stick, slide the long metal spatula underneath to loosen it, and sprinkle both sides of the dough circle with a little flour.

8 Move the baking sheet close to the dough circle. Loosely wrap the dough circle around the rolling pin. Holding the rolling pin, lift the dough over the pie dish. Slowly unroll the dough so it covers the dish and hangs over the edges.

9 Using your fingertips, gently press the dough into the dish. Pile the apple filling into the dough-lined dish and set aside.

10 Repeat the rolling procedure in steps 6 and 7 with the second dough disk. Roll the second dough circle around the rolling pin and transfer it to the top of the filled pie dish as in step 8.

11 Press together the edges of the top and bottom dough circles. Using the scissors or a table knife, cut away the excess dough, leaving a 1-inch border. Roll the border of the dough under itself so that it rests on top of the dish rim.

12 To pinch the edges of the dough together, use your thumb and forefinger of one hand and your forefinger from the other. Gently push and pinch in with your thumb and forefinger at the same time you gently push out with your other forefinger. Pinch all around the pie edge with your thumb and forefingers. Using the sharp knife, cut 3 small slits in the top crust.

13 Bake the pie on the baking sheet until the top is browned and the apples are tender, about 1 hour. Test the pie by inserting a knife in one of the slits and into an apple slice. The knife should glide easily into the slice. Ask an adult to help with the doneness test. Using oven mitts, carefully remove the pie on the baking sheet from the oven and cool the whole thing on the rack until ready to serve. The apple pie is best when served warm. Top each slice with a dollop of sweetened whipped cream, if you like.

Makes 10 servings

sweetened whipped cream

EQUIPMENT

- ❏ **measuring cups & spoons**
- ❏ **medium mixing bowl**
- ❏ **electric mixer**

INGREDIENTS

1½ **cups heavy cream, well chilled**

3 **tablespoons sugar**

1 **teaspoon vanilla extract**

1 In the mixing bowl, combine the cream, sugar, and vanilla. Using the electric mixer set on low speed, begin beating the cream, gradually increasing the speed to high. Beat until soft peaks form, about 2 minutes. To test, turn off the mixer and lift the beaters. If the cream makes soft little peaks that flop over slightly, it is ready. Do not overbeat, or the cream may separate.

2 Use the whipped cream immediately, or cover and refrigerate for up to 2 hours.

Makes 3 cups whipped cream

EQUIPMENT

- ❑ measuring spoons
- ❑ cutting board
- ❑ sharp knife
- ❑ electric blender

- ❑ small bowl
- ❑ 2 ice-cube trays
- ❑ rubber spatula

frozen fruit crush*

INGREDIENTS

2   large, ripe mangoes

1   lemon

3   tablespoons sugar

1 Set 1 mango with flat end down on the cutting board. Using the knife, cut it in half lengthwise just slightly off from the center, avoiding the large pit. Turn the mango around and cut the other side away from the pit. Working with one-half at a time, carefully make a series of cuts through the flesh down to, but not through, the skin, spacing the cuts about 1 inch apart. Give the mango a half turn and make cuts again to create a crosshatch design. Press your fingers against the skin side and push the pulp up. Cut the chunks of fruit away from the skin. Repeat with other half. Repeat entire process with the other mango.

2 Pile the mango chunks into the container of the blender. Cut the lemon in half across the middle. Using one hand, squeeze one-half into a small bowl. Measure out 1 tablespoon juice and add it to the blender with the sugar. Place the lid securely on the blender. Make sure it's on tight! Hold down the lid with your hand and turn the blender on to high speed. Blend until the fruit is thick and smooth.

3 Pour the purée evenly into the ice-cube trays, using the rubber spatula to scrape it all out. Freeze until hard.

4 Place the fruit cubes in the container of the blender. Place the lid securely on the blender, and turn it on to medium speed. Blend, stopping to scrape down the sides of the blender with the spatula, until crushed. Spoon into bowls.

Makes 2 servings

to make another flavor, use 4 cups of your favorite juicy fruit

chocolate chip cookies
and chocolate milk make
a great combination

- ❑ measuring cups & spoons
- ❑ 2 large baking sheets
- ❑ aluminum foil
- ❑ mixing bowls

- ❑ table fork
- ❑ electric mixer
- ❑ rubber spatula
- ❑ table spoon

- ❑ oven mitts & cooling racks
- ❑ metal spatula

chockfull-of-chips cookies

INGREDIENTS

1	cup all-purpose flour
1½	teaspoons baking powder
¼	teaspoon salt
¼	cup (½ stick) butter, at room temperature
¼	cup vegetable shortening
½	cup firmly packed dark brown sugar
½	cup granulated sugar
1	egg
¾	teaspoon vanilla extract
1½	cups semisweet chocolate chips

1 Preheat the oven to 350°F. Line the 2 baking sheets with aluminum foil.

2 In a small mixing bowl, combine the flour, baking powder, and salt. Using the table fork, stir together the ingredients until well blended.

3 In a large mixing bowl, combine the butter, shortening, brown sugar, and granulated sugar. Using the electric mixer set on medium speed, beat the mixture until it is smooth. Turn off the mixer a few times so you can scrape down the sides of the bowl with the rubber spatula. Add the egg and vanilla and continue to beat on medium speed until well blended. Add the flour mixture. Using the rubber spatula, stir until the flour is almost mixed in. Pour in the chips and stir until completely blended.

4 Using the table spoon, drop the batter in mounds onto the foil-lined baking sheets, spacing the mounds about 1½ inches apart.

5 Place 1 baking sheet in the oven and bake the cookies until they are golden brown, 12 to 14 minutes. Using oven mitts, remove the baking sheet from the oven and set it on a rack to cool for about 10 minutes. Carefully slide the metal spatula under each cookie and transfer it to another rack to cool. Repeat with the second baking sheet. You can store the cookies in an airtight container for up to 1 week.

Makes about 3 dozen cookies

- ❏ measuring cups & spoons
- ❏ 8-inch springform cake pan
- ❏ 2 medium mixing bowls
- ❏ table fork & knife

- ❏ electric mixer & rubber spatula
- ❏ toothpick & oven mitts
- ❏ cooling rack

- ❏ metal spatula
- ❏ large, flat plate
- ❏ aluminum foil
- ❏ icing spatula
- ❏ birthday candles

happy birthday cake

INGREDIENTS

1 tablespoon butter and 2 tablespoons all-purpose flour for greasing and flouring pan

1¾ cups all-purpose flour

2½ teaspoons baking powder

¼ teaspoon salt

½ cup (1 stick) butter, at room temperature

1 cup sugar

2 eggs

1½ teaspoons vanilla extract

⅔ cup milk

2 recipes Creamy Frosting (page 112), chocolate variation

1 Preheat the oven to 350°F. Grease the inside of the cake pan with the 1 tablespoon butter. Sprinkle the 2 tablespoons flour in the pan and shake the pan to coat it evenly with the flour. Turn the pan upside down and tap out any extra flour. Set the pan aside. In a medium mixing bowl, combine the flour, baking powder, and salt. Using the table fork, stir until well blended.

2 In the other medium mixing bowl, combine the ½ cup butter, sugar, eggs, and vanilla. Using the electric mixer set on medium speed, beat the mixture until it is smooth.

3 Add the milk to the butter-sugar mixture. Reduce the speed to low and beat until smooth, stopping to scrape down the sides of the bowl as needed. Add the flour mixture all at once. Using the rubber spatula, stir gently until the batter is completely moistened and combined.

4 Pour the batter into the prepared pan. Bake the cake until the toothpick inserted into the center comes out clean, 45 to 50 minutes. Using oven mitts, remove the pan from the oven and set it on the rack. Let cool for 15 minutes.

5 Run the table knife along the inside edge of the pan to loosen the cake. Spring open the side of the pan. Lift away the side of the pan and let the cake cool completely on the rack.

6 Slip the metal spatula between the cake and the base of the pan. Lift the cake from the base and place the cake on the large, flat plate. Tuck strips of aluminum foil under the edges. Using the icing spatula or table knife, spread the frosting all over the cake. Remove the pieces of foil. Arrange birthday candles on top. Serve immediately or cover loosely with plastic wrap and store at room temperature for up to 1 day.

Makes 8 to 10 servings

light the candles
and let the party begin

- ❏ measuring cups & spoons
- ❏ mixing bowls
- ❏ electric mixer
- ❏ rubber spatula
- ❏ cutting board
- ❏ sharp knife
- ❏ small saucepan
  & small heatproof bowl
- ❏ wooden spoon
- ❏ pot holder

creamy frosting

INGREDIENTS

6 tablespoons (¾ stick) butter, at room temperature

1½ cups confectioners' sugar, sifted if lumpy

2 tablespoons heavy cream

¾ teaspoon vanilla extract

food coloring (optional)

3 ounces unsweetened chocolate, chopped (optional)

1 To make vanilla frosting, in a medium mixing bowl, combine the butter, confectioners' sugar, cream, and vanilla. Using the electric mixer set on low speed, beat until the mixture is smooth. Turn off the mixer several times so you can scrape down the sides of the bowl with the rubber spatula. Use the frosting immediately.

2 To make colored frosting, make the frosting as directed in step 1. Add a drop or two of food coloring to the frosting and mix until thoroughly blended. Alternatively, divide the frosting among 2 or 3 small bowls and mix a different color into each bowl. Use the frosting immediately.

3 To make chocolate frosting, make the frosting as directed in step 1. Fill the small saucepan half full with water. Choose a small, deep heatproof bowl that fits snugly on the saucepan. Be sure the bottom of the bowl does not touch the water. Add the chocolate to the small bowl and set the whole thing (water-filled pan and bowl) over medium heat. Heat the chocolate, stirring with the wooden spoon until it is melted, about 5 minutes. Using the pot holder, remove the pan from the heat. Ask an adult to help you remove the bowl from the saucepan of water. Be careful: The steam is very hot! Set the bowl aside to cool. Stir the melted and cooled chocolate into the frosting until well blended. Use the frosting immediately.

Makes 1 cup frosting

use food coloring to make as many
different colors of frosting as you like

these cupcakes are baked
in ice-cream cones

EQUIPMENT

- measuring cups & spoons
- 12-cup muffin pan
- mixing bowls & table fork
- electric mixer
- rubber spatula
- large spoon
- toothpick
- oven mitts & cooling rack
- small icing spatula

chocolate cupcake cones

INGREDIENTS

10   flat-bottomed waffle cones

1   cup all-purpose flour

⅓   cup unsweetened cocoa powder

1¾   teaspoons baking powder

¼   teaspoon salt

¼   cup (½ stick) butter, at room temperature, cut into pieces

½   cup sugar

1   egg

½   cup milk

1   teaspoon vanilla extract

1   recipe Creamy Frosting (page 112)

colored sprinkles

1 Preheat the oven to 350°F. Check the cones for holes or cracks and replace if necessary. Put each cone into a cup of the muffin pan.

2 In a small mixing bowl, combine the flour, cocoa, baking powder, and salt. Stir with the table fork until blended.

3 In a medium mixing bowl, combine the butter, sugar, and egg. Using the electric mixer set on medium speed, beat until the mixture is lighter in color and no lumps remain, about 2 minutes. Turn off the mixer a few times so you can scrape down the sides of the bowl with the rubber spatula.

4 Add the milk and vanilla. Reduce the speed to low and beat until smooth, stopping to scrape down the sides of the bowl as needed. Add the flour mixture to the butter-sugar mixture all at once. Using the rubber spatula, stir gently until the batter is completely moistened and combined.

5 Using the spoon, place even amounts of the batter, about 3 tablespoons, into each cone. Gently tap the bottom of the cone on your palm to settle the batter.

6 Bake the cupcakes until a toothpick inserted into the center of 1 cake comes out clean, 25 to 28 minutes. Using oven mitts, remove the muffin pan from the oven and set it on the rack. Let cool completely.

7 Using the icing spatula, spread 1 heaping tablespoon of the frosting on each cupcake. Using your fingers, sprinkle the tops with the colored sprinkles. Serve immediately or cover loosely with plastic wrap and store at room temperature for up to 1 day.

Makes 10 cupcakes

puff pastry is made
of hundreds of thin
layers of dough and
puffs as it bakes

- ❏ measuring cups & spoons
- ❏ 2 large baking sheets
- ❏ aluminum foil
- ❏ small saucepan
- ❏ wooden spoon
- ❏ pot holder
- ❏ small mixing bowl
- ❏ table fork & spoon
- ❏ rolling pin & ruler
- ❏ pastry brush
- ❏ sharp knife
- ❏ oven mitts
- ❏ 2 cooling racks
- ❏ metal spatula

cinnamon and sugar swirls

INGREDIENTS

2	tablespoons butter
⅔	cup sugar
1½	teaspoons ground cinnamon
1	sheet frozen puff pastry, 9 by 10½ inches, thawed

1 Preheat the oven to 375°F. Line the 2 baking sheets with aluminum foil. Put the butter in the small saucepan and set it over medium heat. Stir with the wooden spoon until the butter is melted, 1 to 2 minutes. Using the pot holder, remove the pan from the heat and set it aside to cool.

2 In the small mixing bowl, combine ⅓ cup of the sugar and the cinnamon. Stir with the table fork until blended. Sprinkle some of the remaining ⅓ cup sugar on a work surface. Unfold the thawed puff pastry on top of the sugar with one of the short sides facing you. Generously sprinkle more sugar on top of the puff pastry, spreading it with your hand to cover.

3 Using the rolling pin, roll out the pastry. Begin at the center and roll out to the far end. Then roll from the center toward you. After every two passes of the rolling pin, sprinkle the pastry with more sugar, turn the pastry over, and sprinkle with more sugar. Keep rolling in this manner until the pastry is a 10-by-16-inch rectangle.

4 Use the pastry brush to brush the top of the pastry with the melted butter. Then sprinkle with the cinnamon-sugar mixture. Spread the mixture with your hand to cover the pastry evenly and press down gently.

5 Starting from one of the long sides, roll up the pastry, jelly-roll style, stopping just before reaching the end. Press the edge to seal the seam.

6 Place the roll, seam side down, on the work surface. Using the sharp knife, cut the roll into ½-inch-thick slices. Place the slices about 2 inches apart on the baking sheets.

7 Place 1 baking sheet in the oven and bake the cookies until they are a deep golden brown, 12 to 14 minutes. Using oven mitts, remove the baking sheet from the oven and set it on a rack to cool for about 15 minutes. Using the metal spatula, lift the cookies from the foil and transfer to the rack to cool completely. Repeat with the second baking sheet. Serve immediately or store at room temperature in an airtight container.

Makes 32 cookies

EQUIPMENT

❑ measuring cups & spoons ❑ rubber spatula
❑ 1½- or 2-quart mixing bowl ❑ large, round serving
❑ plastic wrap   plate with a lip
❑ large table spoon ❑ sharp knife

sherbet bombe

INGREDIENTS

1 teaspoon soft butter
for greasing bowl

1 quart (4 cups)
orange sherbet

1 pint (2 cups) lemon
sherbet

1 pint (2 cups)
raspberry sherbet

1 Grease the mixing bowl with the soft butter. Line the bowl with 2 long pieces of plastic wrap, placing the pieces in the shape of a cross. Leave enough plastic wrap hanging over the edges of the bowl to cover the top. Place the bowl in the freezer. Remove the orange sherbet from the freezer and set it on a work surface to soften for about 20 minutes.

2 When the orange sherbet is soft enough to spread, remove the bowl from the freezer and set it on the work surface. Drop spoonfuls of the orange sherbet around the inside of the bowl. Smooth the sherbet with the rubber spatula until it forms an even layer. Return the bowl to the freezer. Remove the lemon sherbet to soften for about 20 minutes.

3 When the lemon sherbet is soft enough to spread and the orange sherbet is firm, remove the bowl from the freezer. Drop spoonfuls of the lemon sherbet over the orange layer. Spread as directed in step 2. Return the bowl to the freezer. Remove the raspberry sherbet to soften for about 20 minutes.

4 When the raspberry sherbet is soft enough to spread and the lemon sherbet is firm, remove the bowl from the freezer. Drop spoonfuls of the raspberry sherbet into the center and smooth the top. Fold the plastic wrap over the top to cover. Freeze until hard, about 6 hours.

5 To serve, have the plate ready. Remove the bowl from the freezer and peel back the plastic wrap from the top. Turn the bowl over onto the plate. Lift the edge of the bowl with one hand to loosen the bombe from it. Remove the bowl and peel off all the plastic wrap. Ask an adult to help you cut the bombe into wedges, using the knife dipped in hot tap water.

Makes 8 servings

a bombe is a bomb-shaped
French frozen dessert

EQUIPMENT

- ❏ measuring cups & spoons
- ❏ sharp knife & cutting board
- ❏ small plate
- ❏ baking sheet
- ❏ aluminum foil

- ❏ large mixing bowl
- ❏ wooden spoon
- ❏ pastry blender
- ❏ ruler & oven mitts
- ❏ cooling rack

mixed-berry shortcakes

INGREDIENTS

¼ cup solid vegetable shortening, chilled

¼ cup (½ stick) chilled butter

2½ cups all-purpose flour, plus extra for dusting

¼ cup sugar

1 tablespoon baking powder

¾ teaspoon salt

1 cup milk

1 teaspoon vanilla extract

1 recipe Sweetened Whipped Cream (page 105)

2 cups mixed berries, sliced, if necessary, and sweetened lightly with sugar

1 Using the sharp knife, cut the shortening and butter into ½-inch pieces on the cutting board. Pile onto the small plate and set in the refrigerator to keep cold.

2 Preheat the oven to 400°F. Line the baking sheet with aluminum foil and set aside.

3 In the large mixing bowl, combine the flour, sugar, baking powder, and salt. Using the wooden spoon, stir until blended.

4 Drop the butter and shortening pieces into the flour mixture. Using the pastry blender, press down on the ingredients, using many short strokes, until the mixture looks like coarse crumbs with only small pieces of fat still visible.

5 Add the milk and vanilla. Gently stir with the wooden spoon just until the mixture forms a rough, shaggy dough. Dump the dough onto a work surface. Using your fingers, gently press the dough into a 6-by-4-inch rectangle. If your fingers stick to the dough, lightly dust them with flour.

6 Turn the rectangle so a short side is facing you. Using the sharp knife, cut the dough in half lengthwise, to form 2 strips each 2 inches wide by 6 inches long. Cut each strip crosswise into 3 equal squares. Arrange the squares about 3 inches apart on the prepared baking sheet.

7 Bake the shortcakes until the tops are golden brown, 22 to 25 minutes. Using oven mitts, remove the baking sheet from the oven and set it on the rack to cool.

8 When cool enough to handle, split each shortcake and serve with Sweetened Whipped Cream and the berries.

Makes 6 servings

use your favorite berries
for this summertime dessert

glossary

This alphabetical list gives you simple explanations for terms and ingredients you'll find in this cookbook.

a

al dente
Italian for "to the tooth." Used to describe perfectly cooked pasta that is tender but still a bit chewy.

alfalfa sprouts
Little green sprouts grown from alfalfa seeds. They add a crisp texture to salads and sandwiches.

asian sesame oil
Golden brown oil pressed from toasted sesame seeds. Used to season Asian dishes.

b

bake
To cook with hot, dry air in an oven.

baking powder
A powdery white product made by combining baking soda, an acid such as cream of tartar, and cornstarch or flour. Used to make some doughs and batters rise during baking.

beat
To mix ingredients vigorously, stirring with a spoon, fork, or beaters in a circular motion.

blend
To combine two or more ingredients thoroughly. Also, to mix ingredients in an electric blender.

boil
To heat a liquid until bubbles constantly rise to its surface and break. A gentle boil is when small bubbles rise and break slowly. A rapid boil is when large bubbles rise and break quickly.

broth, canned
A liquid rich with the flavors of chicken, meat, seafood, or vegetables.

brown
To cook food until it turns a light golden or dark brown.

c

chocolate
Chocolate is available in many different forms, including semisweet chocolate, a dark, sweet chocolate sold as blocks, bars, and chips; and unsweetened chocolate, a bitter product sold in small squares or blocks with a strong chocolate flavor.

Unsweetened cocoa powder, different from hot cocoa mix because it includes no sugar or milk products, is a fine, bitter powder that carries a strong chocolate flavor.

chop
To cut food into pieces. Finely chopped pieces are small; coarsely chopped pieces are large.

coat
To cover the surface of a food or a piece of equipment with butter, oil, flour, crumbs, or other ingredient.

consistency
How thick or thin, fine or coarse, smooth or lumpy an ingredient or mixture of ingredients is.

couscous, instant
This specialty from Morocco is a tiny form of pasta served like rice.

crush
To press down on an ingredient, such as a garlic clove or a spice seed, to reduce it to a paste or a powder.

d

dissolve
To mix a fine-textured, solid substance, such as sugar or salt, with a liquid until the solid disappears.

divide
To split a batch of dough or batter or individual ingredients into smaller, usually equal batches.

drain
To pour off liquid, leaving solids behind. To do this, the solids and liquid are usually poured into a strainer or colander.

drizzle
To pour liquid or icing over food in a thin stream.

dust
To cover a food, your hands, or a work surface lightly with a powdery substance such as flour or confectioners' sugar.

e

eggs
Sold in a range of sizes. Use eggs marked "large" for the recipes in this book.

f

flip
To turn an ingredient over, usually with a spatula and a quick twist of the wrist.

flour, all-purpose
The most common kind of flour available, composed of a blend of wheats to make it equally reliable for muffins, cakes, cookies, and other baked goods.

flour tortilla
A round, thin, griddle-cooked flat bread that comes from Mexico and the American Southwest.

g

garnish
To decorate a dish before serving. Also, the food used to decorate a dish.

grate
To draw food, such as cheese, across a surface of small, sharp-edged holes on a box grater-shredder.

grease
To rub a pan or baking dish with fat, such as butter or vegetable shortening, to prevent sticking.

h

heat (stove)
A recipe should tell you the heat level to use on the stove top. Heat levels are marked on the dial for each burner. Low heat is usually just above the lowest setting, which recipes sometimes call very low. Medium heat is when the dial is turned on halfway. High heat comes with the dial at its highest setting. Medium-low and medium-high heats are midway between those two settings. Gas burners allow you to see the flame, to help judge the heat level.

i

invert
To turn a piece of cookware, usually a pan containing a cake, upside down so that the food falls gently onto a cooling rack or a dish.

k

knead
To work dough with your hands, using pressing, folding, and turning motions. When dough is fully kneaded, it becomes smooth and elastic.

l

lengthwise
In the same direction as, or parallel to, the longest side of a piece of food or a pan.

line
To cover a pan with aluminum foil, waxed paper, or parchment paper to prevent food from sticking.

m

mash
To break down soft food such as bananas or boiled potatoes by pressing on it with a fork, potato masher, or other tool.

melt
To heat a solid substance, such as butter or chocolate, until it becomes liquid.

mix
To stir together dry or wet ingredients until combined.

p

pinch
The amount of a dry ingredient that you can pick up, or "pinch," between your thumb and forefinger; less than $1/8$ teaspoon.

preheat
To heat an oven to a specific temperature before use.

prick
To make slight indentations, usually with fork tines, in the surface of a food or ingredient such as pastry.

purée
To mash one or more ingredients, by hand or in a blender or food processor, until reduced to a smooth consistency. Also, any ingredient or mixture that has that consistency.

r

reduce (heat)
To turn down the heat under a pan or inside an oven.

refrigerate
To place food in the refrigerator to chill or to become firm.

rise
What happens to a dough or batter when it becomes bigger as a result of the gas released by yeast, baking powder, or baking soda.

roll out
To flatten dough with a rolling pin until it is smooth, even, and usually thin.

room temperature
The temperature of a comfortable room. Butter is often brought to room temperature so it will soften and blend easily.

s

season to taste
To add salt, pepper, or other seasonings to food little by little, stopping and tasting until it is to your liking.

set
When a liquid congeals or a dough or batter becomes more solid as it cooks or cools.

set aside
To put ingredients to one side while you do something else.

shortening, vegetable
A solid fat made from vegetable oil and used in cooking and baking.

shred
To cut an ingredient on the medium or large holes of a box grater-shredder.

simmer
To cook a liquid at just below the boiling point. The surface should be barely bubbling.

slice
To cut food lengthwise or crosswise with a knife, forming thick or thin pieces.

snip
To cut delicate ingredients such as fresh herbs into tiny pieces, usually with kitchen scissors.

soften
To let an ingredient such as butter sit at room temperature until soft enough to spread.

spread
To apply a soft mixture or ingredient such as frosting or butter over another food in an even layer.

steam
To cook food with the hot steam that rises from boiling water. The food is usually held in a rack above the water.

stir
To move a spoon, fork, whisk, or other utensil continuously through dry or wet ingredients, usually in a circular pattern.

stir-fry
An Asian cooking method in which small pieces of food are quickly stirred and tossed in a large, deep pan over high heat.

sugar
The three most common sugars are granulated sugar, small, white granules that pour easily; brown sugar, a moist blend of granulated sugar and molasses; and confectioners' sugar, which is granulated sugar finely ground with a small amount of cornstarch.

t

tender
Describes food that is cooked until soft enough to cut and chew easily but is not mushy.

thicken
When a food changes from a loose, liquid consistency to a thick, firm one.

tofu
Also called bean curd, this Asian ingredient is made from cooked soybeans crushed to a milky liquid, curdled, and then pressed into blocks. It has a smooth texture and mild flavor.

toss
To mix ingredients by tumbling them together with your hands, two forks, or two spoons.

trim
To cut food so that it is uniform in size and shape. Also, to cut away any unneeded or inedible part.

v

vanilla extract
A liquid flavoring made from vanilla beans, the dried pods of a type of orchid.

vermicelli
An Italian term, meaning "little worms," for very thin spaghetti strands.

w

whisk
To stir a liquid such as cream or egg whites vigorously with a whisk, adding air and thereby increasing its volume.

work surface
A flat space used for cutting, mixing, or preparing foods.

y & z

yeast, quick-rise
Microscopic plants known as yeasts make breads rise. In recent years, quick-rise yeasts have been developed to make breads rise in only half the usual time.

zest
The thin, brightly colored outer layer of peel of a citrus fruit. It is most often grated or cut into pieces.

equipment glossary

electric mixer
Handheld mixer with different speeds quickly mixes batters and doughs.

frying pans
For frying all kinds of food on top of the stove.

jelly-roll pan
A baking sheet with four sides. These pans are used in sweet and savory baking.

pastry brushes
For brushing butter and glazes on dough.

pot holders
Thick, heavy-duty cotton protects hands when handling hot pots or pans.

box grater-shredder
For grating citrus zest and for shredding cheese.

cups for measuring liquids
Cups used to measure liquids are transparent so you can line up the amount of any liquid with the correct measurement marked on the side.

cups for measuring dry ingredients
Dry-ingredient measuring cups hold an exact amount and have straight rims so you can level off the ingredients.

potato masher
Makes it easy to smash boiled potatoes.

rubber spatula
For scraping the sides of mixing bowls.

saucepans with lids
Pans of different sizes for stove-top cooking such as simmering sauces, boiling pasta, and cooking rice.

sharp knives
Large, sharp knives are for slicing, dicing, chopping, and mincing all sorts of ingredients. Small, sharp knives are for peeling and coring. Handle with care!

spoons for measuring
These spoons are used to measure exact, small amounts of both dry and liquid ingredients. Their rims are straight so you can level off dry ingredients precisely.

springform pan
Cake pan with removable sides makes it easy to remove delicate baked goods.

strainer
For making dry ingredients powdery smooth and for draining liquid from solids.

vegetable peelers
For stripping off vegetable peels.

wooden spoon
Because it doesn't get hot, a wooden spoon with a long handle is the best choice for stirring foods while they cook.

index

OXMOOR HOUSE INC.
Oxmoor House books are distributed by Sunset Books,
80 Willow Road, Menlo Park, CA 94025
Phone: (650) 321-3600   Fax: (650) 324-1532

Vice President/General Manager: **Rich Smeby**
Director of Special Sales: **Gary Wright**

Oxmoor House and Sunset Books are divisions of
Southern Progress Corporation

WILLIAMS-SONOMA
Founder and Vice-Chairman: **Chuck Williams**
Book Buyer: **Cecilia Michaelis**

WELDON OWEN INC.
Chief Executive Officer: **John Owen**
President: **Terry Newell**
Chief Operating Officer: **Larry Partington**
Vice President International Sales: **Stuart Laurence**
Associate Publisher: **Val Cipollone**
Copy Editor: **Sharon Silva**
Consulting Editor: **Norman Kolpas**
Designer: **Anne Galperin**
Production Editor: **Kathryn Meehan**
Food Stylist: **Dan Becker**
Prop Stylist: **Carol Hacker**
Studio Assistant: **Sheri Giblin**
Food Styling Assistant: **Michael Procopio**
Equipment Photography: **Chris Shorten**

Printed in Hong Kong by Midas Printing Ltd.

acknowledgments

Weldon Owen would like to thank Stephanie Sherman, Chris Hemesath,
Desne Border, and Ken DellaPenta for their valuable assistance in
producing this book. We would also like to thank our wonderful kid
models, James Blose and Katie Sugarman.

Abby Dodge would like to thank her mother, Margaret Gordon Johnson,
for encouraging her youthful forays into the culinary arts and for enjoying
(or at least pretending to) every single effort; and her chief recipe testers:
Abigail Lupoff, Alissa Smith, Alexa Tilghman, Charlie Van Kirk, and Alex
and Tierney Dodge for their wonderful insights and suggestions. Their
enthusiastic testing and tasting made these recipes the best ever!

Williams-Sonoma *The Kid's Cookbook*
conceived and produced by Weldon Owen Inc.
814 Montgomery Street, San Francisco, CA 94133

In collaboration with Williams-Sonoma
3250 Van Ness Avenue, San Francisco, CA 94109

A WELDON OWEN PRODUCTION

Library of Congress Cataloging-in-Publication Data is available

ISBN 0-8487-2607-3

5 6 7 8 9 10

Abby at age 10

abigail johnson dodge

is a Paris-trained author, culinary instructor, and pastry chef. She has been an editor at *Woman's Day* and *Parents* magazines, and currently directs the test kitchen for *Fine Cooking* magazine. Dodge is the author of *Great Fruit Desserts*, was a contributor to the *All New All-Purpose Joy of Cooking* and *Cookies for Christmas*, and created *Cooking in the Classroom*, an elementary school program that teaches kids how to cook. Her own young son and daughter, Alex and Tierney, are enthusiastic cooks and tasters, especially if the samples are chocolate.

Chuck at age 12

chuck williams

has helped to revolutionize cooking in America. He opened his first store in the California wine country town of Sonoma in 1956, later moving it to San Francisco. More than 150 stores are now open in the United States, and the company's catalog has an annual circulation of over 42 million. The philosophy behind his success is aptly summed up by the title of the cookbook he wrote to chronicle Williams-Sonoma's first 40 years: *Celebrating the Pleasures of Cooking*.

Leigh at age 9

leigh beisch

is an award-winning photographer and an alumna of the Rhode Island School of Design. Her work frequently appears in national advertisements, magazines, and cookbooks. She lives in San Francisco.